HRD
SURVIVAL
SKILLS

HRD

SURVIVAL
SKILLS

**Essential strategies to
promote training and
development within
your organization**

Gulf Publishing Company
Houston, Texas

Jessica Levant

HRD Survival Skills

Gulf Publishing Company
Book Division
P.O. Box 2608 □ Houston, Texas 77252-2608

10 9 8 7 6 5 4 3 2 1

Library of Congress Cataloging-in-Publication Data
Levant, Jessica
    HRD survival skills : essential strategies to promote training and development within your organization / Jessica Levant.
        p.   cm. — (Improving human performance series)
    Includes bibliographical references (p.   ) and index.
    ISBN 0-88415-270-7 (alk. paper)
    1. Marketing.   2. Employees—Training of—Marketing.
3. Education—Marketing.   I. Title.   II. Series.
HF5415.L4756   1998
658.3′ 12404—dc21   98-15721
                                                           CIP

Printed on Acid-Free Paper (∞)

Contents

Acknowledgments

I could not have written this book without the influence of several very special colleagues. The first acknowledgment goes to the late Dugan Laird, whose common-sense approach to the theory and practice of training and development formed my thinking years ago and has never gone out-of-date. I continue to lend his book, *Approaches to Training and Development,* to colleagues who approach me for advice on coming to grips with this profession. The other posthumous thanks goes to Tony Newby, my friend and challenger of many years, and the one who inspired me to put pen to paper in the first place.

I wish to thank those who read, commented, contributed "Cases in Point," answered my unending questions, and generally made the work possible: Michael Manion, Harvey Lifton, Irene Antipa, Charles Atthill, John Lingvall, and in the early days, David Cleeton, Ann Nixon, Philip Cooper, Elizabeth Ward, Peter Marsh, Jim Stadelmaier, Naomi Stanford, and Brenda Hazlewood. To my Gulf Publishing Company editors, Kristine Fahrenholz and Joyce Alff, goes much appreciation for their patience and extremely fast responses to my constant stream of e-mails, blotting out the geographical restrictions to our communication.

And finally, special thanks to many of my own clients whose stories appear (mostly in disguise) throughout the book.

Preface

The topic of this book, *connecting* with the customers of training and performance improvement programs, has been of great interest to me for many years. As an external consultant, I have been in many organizations and have seen many well-planned programs go awry because the training and development department, while working to a high professional standard, got more involved in the "product" and its design than with meeting the actual need(s) of the client. Often, I observed glaring omissions from companies' training programs. Sometimes they were more subtle, but the fact remained: these organizations were overlooking an essential ingredient of training and development programs. That ingredient encompasses a body of knowledge and activity geared to connecting with the customer; it comes under the general heading of MARKETING.

It has been said before that HRD professionals are not always comfortable with the business side of things. While I believe that is changing, I have found that professionals engaged in developing and improving individual and organizational performance remain at odds with the idea of marketing—it sounds a bit crass, like selling or advertising. Yet, if the contribution trainers and training managers make to their organizations, whether directly or through line managers and team leaders, is not effectively marketed within the organization, there is a real danger of the efforts being unnoticed, unappreciated, unsubscribed and, eventually, undone.

Monumental effort often goes into establishing performance improvement endeavors within organizations. There are time-consuming needs analyses, clarification of specific corporate objectives, frequent consultations with department heads and managers, cautious assessment and engagement of "culture matching" external providers, and painstaking planning of the appropriate solution. In the case of training, this is then followed with well-thought-out designs; the search for the right exercise, case study, or other solution; expensive visuals; and possibly lengthy negotiations with training facilities. Yet, these necessary components often do not ensure sufficient success of the endeavor.

An expensively planned training program may play to a handful of participants—or not at all. A meeting to brainstorm ideas or carve the way forward is devoid of motivation. A new performance appraisal system goes unsubscribed. In sum, much of the good work done is wasted; often careers falter and whole departments are cut, simply because what is done is not *seen* to be needed.

Marketing means staying visible—even after you've gathered your information. It means constantly taking the "customer's" temperature. It means keeping the customer involved during all phases of development and spreading the word about the value that training adds to potential customers throughout the organization.

I wrote this book for those whose job it is to provide or manage the training and performance improvement programs within an organization. It is designed to help the reader develop essential thinking and techniques for continual customer focus.

This book presents practical guidelines for identifying, assessing, and attracting your market. It includes ways to focus on the image you project as a training and development department (or whatever name it enjoys in your organization) and methods for getting that right. It suggests how to develop and maintain positive visibility. Above all, this book is intended to be practical. It is full of ideas and ways to generate more ideas to bring this "common sense" into "common practice."

As you read, you will come across several "For You to Think About" boxes, which are intended to give you the opportunity to consider, quite specifically, what steps you have already taken and which ones you need to take. The questions may lead you into areas you have not considered before. It will be worth your while to take the time to answer them.

There are also activities to help you build your own customer connection strategies. Many of these exercises will be appropriate for team effort and could easily form the basis of team meetings.

I hope that the "Cases in Point" will be instructive. While all situations have in fact occurred, in order to avoid any embarrassment, I have made certain changes in detail to protect the identity of the organization or people involved.

CHAPTER 1

Shifting the Focus

This book does not start from the beginning. It assumes that the reader does not have to be convinced that training and development programs play a very important role in an organization's current performance and future prosperity. It also assumes that the reader agrees that high-quality training and development efforts are important in attracting, developing, and retaining high-quality people. In short, it is not a book about how to "do" training and development; rather it is about how the customer connection must underline all training and development efforts throughout the organization for it to stay viable.

THE SYSTEMATIC APPROACH

Because developing client-focused training must be built into basic training and development skills, we will start with a brief review of the systematic approach for creating performance improvement initiatives. The systematic approach is usually presented as the backbone of any competently planned training and development course. This review will allow us to clarify the concepts and techniques referred to throughout this book, and ensure we start from a common understanding. Though the actual words may vary from one organization to the next, the systematic approach generally looks something like Figure 1-1.

One of the problems with this model, as it is presented to most training and development students, is that it is necessary but not sufficient. While it may be the foundation upon which training and devel-

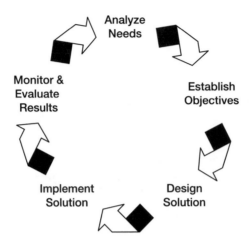

Figure 1-1. The systematic approach.

opment skills are built, and a practical and logical model for provision of performance improvement solutions, it is an *internal* model—it encompasses the tasks that must be performed within the organization to get the "product" right, but does not incorporate how to *engage various customers* in those tasks. When performance improvement efforts are looked at from this perspective, they are like any other product or service—a microwave oven, a personal pension plan, a telephone charge card, even two-surface window cleaners. It could be the greatest idea since sliced bread, only people don't know what it will do, how good it is, how it will actually benefit them, and possibly that it even exists until a vital connection is made between the provider and the intended recipient. It is through the marketing process that the customer learns enough to want to know more about the product, thereby creating a "market."

In training and development, the marketing process should be a transparent overlay on the systematic approach previously described. There are activities which should be attended to every step of the way.

OVERLAYING THE MARKETING PROCESS

Every marketing process starts with identifying potential customers and then learning what the customer population wants—the market research phase. This is not the same as a one-time survey of training needs. It involves personal attention, diagnostic listening, face-to-face contact, and repeated reaching out to learn what customers need *from their point of view*. It also means *really understanding* both the business as a whole and the particular customer's context in order to devise an appropriate solution and to alert them to the possibility of something being developed to meet their need(s). Achieving situations that give this level of personal attention often rests on how the training and development function portrays its image to the rest of the organization.

Marketing efforts of an internal service depend a great deal on image for their continued success. Part of the necessary ongoing market research is to assess the image the rest of the organization has of the training and development function and to determine the "right" image to promote. Visibility only helps if it is positive! (You can use the Training Image Survey on pages 76–77 and 131–132 to assess how your organization perceives the training and development function.)

During the design phase of any training and development solution, there is a need to maintain and strengthen client relationships in order to assess changes in needs and wants and to attend to other influencing factors, for example changes in organizational direction, new managers, etc. This purposeful contact enables the design to stay on target, works to keep customer awareness alive, and maintains "visibility." This personal attention phase allows the introduction of appropriate promotional activity so that when it is time to launch the planned program, customers are eager to participate. This kind of effort is needed on a regular basis to constantly review products and markets.

The next phase is just as crucial: openness to feedback, demonstration of concern to get it right and to continue getting it right, flexibility, and the ability to adapt in a timely manner all come together to ensure that what is provided continues to meet the needs of the customers. This is the phase in which image is tested. What you are and what you are seen to be come together to determine your ongoing viability as a training function.

Later chapters will cover in detail the different marketing processes. For now, it will be useful to look more closely at how the systematic approach is normally followed.

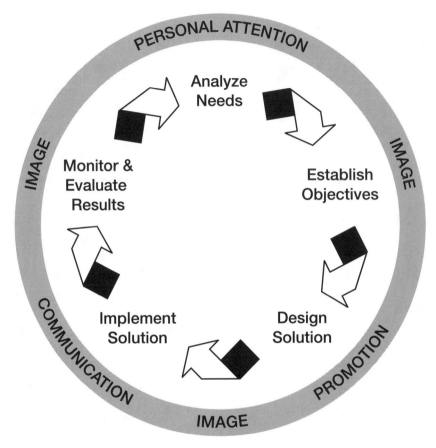

Figure 1-2. The marketing process cycle.

Performance Analysis

Let's start with analyzing performance needs. We know that performance should

- ❏ Be driven by the business needs (start with the corporate mission)
- ❏ Have the support of the top executive
- ❏ Look at current and future gaps in performance throughout the organization

❑ Take into account individual needs and preference wherever practicable

❑ Be focused on improving current organization's performance

However, the reality is sometimes a bit different.

A needs analysis is often a paper-intensive process, whether through questionnaires or as a result of performance appraisal systems. Occasionally an external consultant is brought in to do a "complete analysis"—often after none has been done for some time, or as a requirement for some outside funding of training. In that case, there tends to be a comprehensive document delineating what training or other performance improvement solution every segment of the organization needs.

Sometimes the analysis involves the entire staff; more often a particular group (e.g., customer service staff, managers, or department heads). Performance improvement needs are either expressed in current terms or predicted for future identified competencies. They are frequently presented in broad terms (e.g., supervisory skills, communication or presentation skills, etc.). When time, authority, and normal practice permit, the dedicated HRD professional will have face-to-face conversations with at least some of the population to gain a more specific picture of needs. (For a full exploration of the Needs Analysis process, see Further Reading.)

There is nothing inherently wrong with any of these techniques. Depending on the thoroughness of the investigation, a more or less comprehensive set of performance improvement needs will be collected which will be the focus of attention for the next period of time. From a marketing perspective, however, there are other considerations, such as

❑ How you introduced the needs analysis

❑ How and when you followed up, and what message(s) that gave

❑ Whose jargon you used—that of the business itself or the more esoteric "*HR-speak*"

❑ If the process was paper-based, what image the document created of the training and development department

❑ How customer involvement in the process was encouraged

❑ What expectations the needs analysis generated

FOR YOU TO THINK ABOUT . . .

What steps do you usually take to analyze performance needs?

What are the "image implications" that the needs analysis process creates of the training and development function?

Where, specifically, in the needs analysis process could you enhance customer relations?

Objective Setting

Once you analyze performance needs, you can set specific objectives. Ask yourself what types of outcomes are needed and by whom.

While learning objectives are important, what is crucial is the impact achievement of those objectives will have on the business unit and the organization as a whole.

It is all too easy for the performance improvement professional to overlook the customer at this stage—especially the line manager. You can prevent this by seeking direct involvement of key players, which will help generate ownership and commitment to the forthcoming solution and will help promote it using language that will attract participation. For example, you can

- ❑ Ask line managers to contribute or comment on objectives
- ❑ Organize interviews or group forums to discuss progress on performance improvement initiatives and review expected outcomes
- ❑ Obtain actual descriptions of what will be different if objectives are met
- ❑ Circulate draft proposals, inviting comment
- ❑ Check that a clear message is given that customer opinions are valued

Designing the Solution

It is normal at this stage for the training staff to "go underground"—to work very hard selecting or designing, or causing to be designed, the appropriate activity to improve the chosen performance. Often there are long periods of silence with no customer contact. The training staff will spend much time looking at options, costing the projects, and planning the development. In the case of a training solution, the staff will focus on designing the learning activities, preparing materials, booking facilities, organizing schedules, and attending to all the details to make the programs successful. And if you're lucky, they will be.

More commonly, once you implement the training, several of the following consequences may arise, causing obvious difficulties, if you do not sufficiently market the training function:

❑ Too few training participants to cover expenses

❑ Last-minute rescheduling because of conflict with other events

❑ Unanticipated cancellations, substitutions, and no-shows

❑ Insufficient information available to participants about level and content of course

❑ Repetitious, time-consuming phone calls requesting course descriptions

❑ Participants arriving without the appropriate prerequisites or without completing pre-course assignments

❑ Confusion over training location, start-up time, etc.

❑ Participant complaints about arrangements, location, dates, and times

❑ Early departures and late arrivals due to conflicts with other meetings or activities

❑ Not enough participants to generate stimulating discussions, adequate group work, etc.

The previously listed items are used by permission of the American Society of Training and Development [1].

Other problems you may encounter involve the inappropriate use of external courses. When managers do not know what the organization is offering (or can offer), employees may be sent to external programs—often less relevant and at a higher cost. Frequently, the course won't match employees' needs as well as the internal course would have, and sometimes the terminology will confuse them. To compound this issue, often managers of different departments attend different external courses on similar topics, e.g., problem-solving and decision-making. The results are inconsistent practices within the organization and difficulties in supporting work application and further development of the learning. External course offerings are not intrinsically wrong, but without thinking through the actual employee needs and future work application(s) of the learning, it is quite possible to create performance confusion rather than performance improvement.

THE CONSEQUENCES OF NOT BEING CUSTOMER-FOCUSED

When your training program is not customer-focused, there can be and usually are a range of serious consequences, such as the following:

❑ *Detriment to learning for*

Participants who were ill-prepared, came late or left early

Participants who had to bide time because of other participants

Participants who must endure repetition for the above groups

Participants in groups that are too small for useful exchange of ideas

❑ *Wasted time and money for*

Training staff who handle unnecessary phone calls to give out last-minute course details

Administrative staff who are often asked to "round up" people to increase training group numbers (this is also a sure-fire way to get reluctant or inappropriate participants)

Trainers and other staff who must spend time waiting for all participants to arrive

❑ *Tarnished reputation and image of the training department because*

Last-minute surprises often leave an unprofessional image

Unsatisfied, confused, or disgruntled participants tell other would-be participants not to bother with the training program

❏ *Bottom line*

More trainers than are necessary must be scheduled

External contractors will require cancellation fees

The training program budget for the following year may be reduced because of all the cancellations the previous year

In the worst cases, the whole training function can be on the line (see following Case in Point).

FOR YOU TO THINK ABOUT . . .

Which of the problem situations ring true for you?

What are the potential consequences to your organization?

Case in Point

Richard was the training and development director for an international bank. He reported directly to top management and had a good working relationship with three of the five people in the top management team. He was often asked to contribute ideas. He therefore felt confident with his knowledge of the corporate direction and strategy.

He was well liked by managers throughout the 2,500-person organization and was welcomed into their offices when he came to chat about their training needs. He had *carte blanche* from top management for his decisions regarding training and, as the bank had been doing quite well, he did not have financial constraints.

He believed that to keep the "edge," the training department should be small, and external consultants—selected for their particular experience and "fit" with the organization—should be brought in to tailor training solutions to specific needs as they were identified. He used several such consultants and developed good relationships with all of them. He was open about the organization and eager for the consultants to feel they understood the bank's culture. He expected and received training content—exercises, examples, case studies, etc.— that were relevant to the bank.

He produced quarterly training calendars that listed all the various offerings, whether classroom courses, CBT, or project-based training. He sent these to all the bank's managers.

Richard insisted that potential participants complete pre-training questionnaires indicating why they were interested in a particular type of training and what their individual objectives were. These had to be signed by their managers. Richard also circulated follow-up questionnaires to look at how the participants applied what they learned from training to their actual work. Most post-training comments were positive and trainers were responsive to any suggestions for improvement.

Three years after taking the position as training and development director, Richard's job was eliminated.

ACTIVITY

Test Your Marketing Sense

What types of marketing intervention can you think of that could have been employed to this training director's advantage?

1. _____

2. _____

3. _____

4. _____

5. _____

6. _____

7. _____

8. _____

9. _____

10. _____

In the previous case, the training director clearly paid good attention to the "basics." He followed the systematic approach: assessing needs; designing, evaluating, and revising learning activities to suit participant needs; thus resulting in participants applying in the workplace what they had learned and a high level of acceptance among participants and their managers. The training director was aware of the need to provide timely, relevant professional training, which he provided and modified to match the organization's changing practices. So what went wrong? It can never be known for certain, but clearly some deficiencies in basic marketing are visible. If you return to this Case in Point after reading the rest of the book, you should be able to list several actions Richard should have taken.

Evaluation of Training

It will be no surprise that monitoring and evaluating the outcomes of training are not as frequently attended to as they should be. Though five levels of evaluation have been identified (see Figure 1-3) [2], the majority of organizations rely on only two levels: end-of-course "reactionnaires" and the following year's performance appraisals. A few attempt to review employees' performance indicators some time after the performance intervention has been completed, and occasionally external consultants have been brought in to do a broadscale evaluation of the organization's efforts to improve performance. As has been repeatedly documented, very few organizations attempt to track how training impacts the overall organizational performance or the actual return on investment. A notable exception, and hopefully an indicator of future trends, is the performance consultancy model developed at Pacific Gas & Electric. There, "performance consultants" measure the success of their employee-performance solutions by the money saved by their clients as a direct result of their endeavors.

This is not the place to discuss how to best evaluate the training and development or other performance solutions you design; there are excellent books on the topic, some of which are listed in Further Reading. Yet, we are constantly reminded that high-performing organizations are continually collecting customer satisfaction data and using it to improve their product. It is no different for the high-performing training and development function [3]. From a marketing

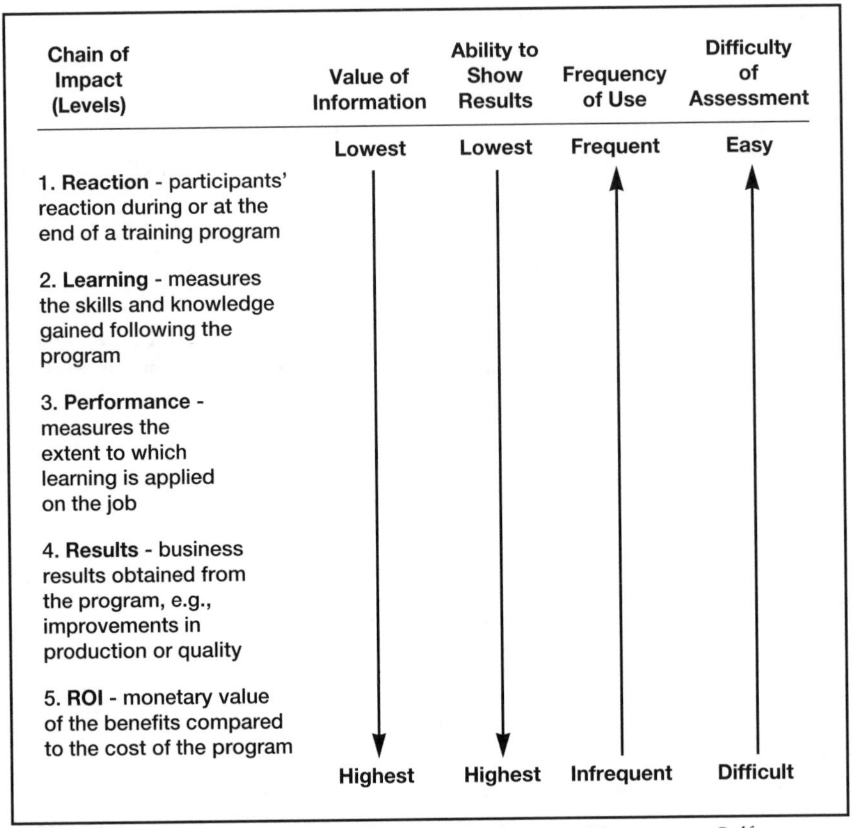

Chain of Impact (Levels)	Value of Information	Ability to Show Results	Frequency of Use	Difficulty of Assessment
	Lowest	Lowest	Frequent	Easy
1. **Reaction** - participants' reaction during or at the end of a training program				
2. **Learning** - measures the skills and knowledge gained following the program				
3. **Performance** - measures the extent to which learning is applied on the job				
4. **Results** - business results obtained from the program, e.g., improvements in production or quality				
5. **ROI** - monetary value of the benefits compared to the cost of the program				
	Highest	Highest	Infrequent	Difficult

Adapted from Phillips, J. J., *Accountability in Human Resource Management,* Gulf Publishing Co., 1996.

Figure 1-3. *Levels of evaluation.*

point of view, however, monitoring and evaluation activities can provide another beneficial point of contact with the training and development customer. Monitoring and evaluation activities also play a key role in helping the training and development function test how the approach used operates in relation to the image you are trying to promote. For example, it is possible to make some inferences about the way in which the training function is perceived and make comparisons with historical data.

The benchmark is an enhancement of reputation and image from *every* initiative. Don't overlook, also, the value of reviewing your marketing effort at each stage. For example, how effectively do your trainers work to enhance the *position* of training and development in the organization?

ACTIVITY

1. Review the *processes* you use to deliver performance improvement solutions. For each process, consider your relationship with the training program's customer. How much customer contact was there during

❏ Needs analysis

_____

_____

❏ Objective setting

_____

_____

❏ Design

_____

_____

❏ Implementation

_____

_____

❏ Evaluation

_____

_____

2. What *marketing activities* have you engaged in over the past year?

1. _____

2. _____

3. _____

4. _____

5. _____

THE COMPLETE TRAINING AND DEVELOPMENT EQUATION

It seems reasonable to posit that well-designed, effective training and development solutions meet two essential criteria:

1. **Quality (Q)** refers to such things as the method of delivery, competence of trainers or other experts, accuracy of materials, administration and resource management—those things which make up "best practice," so that your organization's performance improvement initiatives keep pace with or exceed those of the competition. While there may sometimes be cause for quick fixes and off-the-shelf—even occasionally off-the-cuff solutions—you won't be cementing an image of quality with these.

2. **Relevance (R)** means what you are offering relates to the customer-perceived need and drives corporate performance. In this context, "customer" refers not only to the direct recipients of your training and development programs, but to the organization as a whole. Dependent on alignment with corporate goals, strategy, and culture, relevance to the customer includes such factors as timeliness, targeting the right people, developing essential skills, and delivery within appropriate formats and time frames.

   Quality and relevance are reflected in the ability to anticipate the organization's future needs and to plan training and development initiatives that directly influence its performance. But these criteria alone are not enough to ensure that providing training and development solutions is sustainable within the organization.

3. **Marketability (M)** is a third element that is also needed for this sustainability. Marketability is the extent to which the contribution made by the training and development function is perceived by its customers as adding value to the organization—effectively, your "desirability." This positive perception presupposes that the customer knows of its existence in the first place.

Sustainable training and development activity, then, can be represented by the formula

$$S = Q + R + M$$

If any of the elements are low, so is the sustainability of the training and development provision. Marketing, therefore, is absolutely essential for training and development to be effective over the longer term. It is an equal partner to quality and relevance. That is why marketing is not a choice but a necessity.

To build a mutually satisfying and beneficial link between the training and development function and the rest of the organization, you must be *seen* to be demonstrating an underlying and pervasive customer focus, total involvement in the business, and a personal commitment to providing the right solutions.

The rest of this book will help you come to grips with the "what" and the "how" of establishing this level of customer focus.

SUMMARY

This chapter demonstrated that well-specified and designed training and development are not enough to guarantee a sustainable training and development function. Marketing processes that require a shift of focus to continually include and involve the customer must be embedded throughout the normal practice of planning and developing performance improvement solutions.

Some of the things that go wrong when marketing is not done were exposed, and activities were presented to help the reader analyze past training and development initiatives.

Therefore, this chapter made a case that marketing is necessary, and introduced the basic components of a strategy to produce a sustainable training and development function.

REFERENCES/NOTES

1. Info-Line Issue 605, *How To Market Your Training Programs,* Published by the American Society for Training and Development, May 1986. Used with permission.

2. See Jack J. Phillips, *Accountability in Human Resource Management,* Gulf Publishing Co., 1996.

3. Positioning of training within high-performance organizations was the subject of a 1994 benchmarking study by Coopers & Lybrand. Full report available through the Center of Excellence for Learning Systems, Arlington, VA 22209.

CHAPTER 2

What Marketing Training Means

FOCUS ON THE CONNECTION

Academic and commercial definitions of marketing abound, and this is not the place to weigh them and choose the perfect definition. In all discussions of marketing, however, it is described as a total management process; it has to do with determining demand and it includes stimulating that demand toward your particular offerings. For the purpose of this book then, a useful definition will focus on the connection:

> *Everything you do that is aimed at getting the customer to want what you have to offer.*

This is in itself a definition of marketing *activity*. It does not mention products; it focuses on the customer and the supplier and *the things they do*.

Let's go back to the two-surface window cleaner. Imagine going out into the world with your clipboard and interviewing a 20 percent sample of shoppers in a large supermarket on a Wednesday evening. A few hours later, excited and full of a sense of promise, you return with your questionnaires showing that the number one distaste for housework is in window cleaning. And further, you have learned that this is because of the dirtiness of outdoor grime, the difficulty in reaching it, and the awkwardness of the whole task.

You argue that windows must be cleaned—and we all know how hard it is to find reliable help—so you get your research and development people to investigate the current products on the market. They spend the next three months inventing, developing, and producing a device that eliminates the most loathsome part of the task: the two-surface window cleaner. You get it tested and have the necessary adjustments made getting it as close to perfect as possible, and then, with the "proof" your customer research provided, you convince some appropriate stores to stock your product.

Should you go out and celebrate now because you've just provided the "perfect solution" to a pervasive need? No, you should not. Despite all the time and energy you and your team devoted to working on matching the product to the need, *you forgot to let the potential customers in on the secret.*

ACTIVITY

What steps would you take to get the customer to *want* the window cleaning product?

1. _____

2. _____

3. _____

4. _____

5. _____

Now let's go back to the world of performance improvement.

Getting the Customer to Want . . .

This is not about the "hard sell"—persistent telephone calls, flashy billboards, or coercion. In fact, management guru Peter Drucker is said to have claimed that the purpose of marketing is to make selling superfluous. These types of activities are obviously inappropriate in the context of a human relations-based discipline and not really appreciated in most other contexts. Yet, getting the customer to want what you can offer is what you have to do! In the previous activity, did you think about the following:

- ❑ Letting the people know what you have to offer—issues of communication come into play here—

  to whom should I be communicating?

  how should I communicate?
  (face-to-face, in writing, electronically, word-of-mouth)

  when is the best time?
  (timely, frequent)

  what should I say?
  (style, content)

  where should I say it?
  (journal, brochure, leaflets, etc.)

- ❑ Making sure what you have is what they need—this requires staying in touch, monitoring how the market is changing by understanding what new products or markets it is pursuing or which problems people are trying to solve, and thinking how this affects your customers as well as the business at large.

- ❑ Offering what you have in a way that suits the customer—this is all about getting the context right—

  format

  time

  style

  level of formality, etc.

If these things don't match the contextual needs of the customer, you will not have provided what the customers need.

The most perceptive training and development managers know their organization. They know what is needed and always listen for new developments. As closely aligned partners to the business leaders, they formulate a training and development strategy that meets the organizational needs, but do so knowing that individual appeal is also vital.

This suggests they keep in mind the three essentials that training and development initiatives must meet:

1. **Quality**—the training program is professionally prepared and delivered.
2. **Relevance**—the training adds value to the part of the organization that is targeted by helping individuals to improve their performance; it meets both business and individual needs.
3. **Marketability**—the training is *perceived* as being of the correct quality and relevance for the task.

Why then do so many training plans seem to be "separate" from day-to-day operations? Why do so many people find that making time to attend a training program is often pushed to the bottom of their priority lists? How can a committed training and development manager change the often unconscious perceptions which generate this attitude?

Getting Exposure

The definition of marketing in this book focuses on your customer and what you have to do. Part of this process is a recognition that there are psychological processes involved in successfully marketing training and development or any other internal service which have to do with the more subjective side of things: people's perceptions of you, your team, and your "products."

To get your customers and therefore your organization to derive the benefits you intend—and to keep you a viable function within the organization—you must

❑ Be seen as pro-active in serving your customers

❑ Project the "right" image in the way you do it

Doing the right thing is not good enough. Marketing is very much about getting seen. You must be seen to be doing the right things at the right time in order to be allowed to continue doing them! This is, perhaps, a sad but true fact of organizational life. The second point, projecting the right image, involves being perceived as a person/department worthy of respect within the organization. What makes you "worthy of respect" will differ somewhat from organization to organization, and considerable time will be spent on this topic in Chapter 6. For now, keep in mind that marketing is not "out there," just something you cause to have done, which is somehow separate from the day-to-day business of providing training; it encompasses and pervades what you do, how you do it, who you are, and who you appear to be.

The following quiz will help you think about the broad scope of marketing.

QUIZ

Check the items that are *not* components of marketing.

1. __ Allowing an external consultant to interview line managers

2. __ Introducing yourself to a new employee

3. __ Making presentations at industry or trade association conferences

4. __ Calling a line manager to discuss plans for a training program

5. __ Editing the employee newsletter

6. __ Facilitating a workshop

7. __ Commenting on new organizational policy

8. __ Sponsoring an "open house"

9. __ Sending out post-training questionnaires

10. __ Sending out course administration information

11. __ Producing documents explaining your department's function

12. __ Having a Learning Resource Center

13. __ Facilitating a strategic meeting for the Executive Board

14. __ Running lunchtime video discussion sessions

15. __ Gathering department heads to discuss training needs for the coming year

16. __ Asking a manager to help out with the content or presentation of a program

17. __ Creating a "company style" for handouts

18. __ Publishing a list of contacts in the training department

19. __ Signing up employees for external programs

20. __ Eating lunch in the company restaurant

You may be surprised that the only item that should be checked is number 12. Why? Because the fact of having the center is not marketing—what it looks like, its relevance and quality, how you publicize it, and how its staff, if any, treat those who use it, are all parts of marketing. The decision to have the facility, though probably a very good one, will produce wasted efforts and resources if it is not promoted in an accessible way to your customers.

What should now be clear is that marketing is the statement you make—through word, deed, or design—that reminds people of your service in a way that appeals to them. Even going to lunch may send a message:

"That's the training manager over there—I must speak to him."

"That's the training manager over there— she's very difficult to get hold of."

"That's the training manager over there— he really gets things done!"

"That's the training manager over there— look who she's sitting with!"

FOR YOU TO THINK ABOUT . . .

When people from your organization see you in the corridors or company restaurant, how might they answer the question "who's that?"

"a nice person, who means well and tries hard, but has no power . . ."

"don't know"

"one of the few people who really understands this organization/our division/our problems, etc."

What are the statements that you truly want? What can you do—just through being somewhere and being seen acting in a certain way—to increase, change, or cancel the "messages" you send?

THE MARKETING MIX

No book about marketing can ignore reference to "the marketing mix." The heart of marketing strategy as it is taught to up-and-coming marketing specialists is the "four P's"—product, price, promotion and place (or sometimes position). A fifth "P" could also be added: people. While there is something to say about each of these, to be most useful, they will be incorporated into relevant chapters where they best fit with the marketing of training and development, rather than treated classically as separate subjects. "Product," for example, might seem a redundant issue as this is a book about performance improvement; however, the content and style of the training (or the learning activities) will be dealt with under "packaging" in Chapter 5. If the training and development function provides consulting services, advice, expertise, or problem-solving, however, your image statement (Chapter 6) should incorporate those concepts. Chapter 5 covers "place" in the guise of "environment." Place or positioning, however, has to do with which needs you decide to address and what kind of image you choose to have. "Price" is about value as well as money. Wherever the cost of training comes from, you will have to demonstrate appropriate value. But value is also measured against time and effort. Chapter 3 discusses this in terms of determining your payoff, and also in Chapter 7, which reveals how to keep close to your customer. "Promotion" is about who you are, what you do, and how you advertise those things. We will explore the concept of who you are under image in Chapter 6. How you promote what you do will be the subject of Chapter 7.

"People" is also about who you are, and the choices you make in recruiting or contracting with those people who reflect the quality and relevance of what you are offering. The people you involve in developing and implementing your performance improvement endeavors make unspoken statements about the image of the training and development function. You will find extensive comments on the contributions people make in Chapters 5 through 9, including the marketing implications of using external providers as part of your training provision.

A Word About Advertising

Advertising is simply one of your many marketing tasks. At the risk of over-stressing, however, it is important to remember that you and your departmental staff are constant advertisements—so be sure the messages those "ads" deliver are in tune with your intentions. For example, if your training and development department is engaged in a major change involving a shift of the organization's culture, *do your people model the new values involved?* Chapter 6 devotes a significant amount of space to working on the messages you send.

Case in Point

John is the manager of the management training function at a major oil services company. He was asked to design and implement training programs to revitalize the appraisal skills of managers as part of a performance management system. John formed a small project team of experienced people to design the training. The training was launched on schedule, and well received.

After twelve months, John had still not found time to meet members of his own team to agree on any personal objectives. Disillusioned with their manager's poor commitment to the new process, the trainers began to "opt out" and then eventually subtly broadcasted John's failure to manage his own team. This damaged the training function's reputation and helped strengthen appeals to reduce the scope of John's function by creating a separate management development function in another part of the organization.

Somehow, John was not aware of the messages he was "sending." He was surprised (and not at all pleased) to lose this important part of his operation.

Key Steps to Effective Marketing of Training

More useful than the list of "P's" is a step-by-step list of activities which will focus you and your team on the essentials of effective marketing of training and development.

To get your customers to want what you have (or will develop) to offer, be it training, internal consulting, or two-surface window cleaners, requires a structured and considered planning process. Some things in your plan you will do periodically; others will require constant attention. There is no great mystique about it—mostly it requires a strong sense of commitment, an ability to recognize opportunities, good organizational skills, and energy. Armed with these, you need to work through a series of clear steps. The following list comprises key areas for attention:

❑ Define your market—identify your customers

❑ Choose your focus—establish where to put competing needs and resources

❑ Strive to build and develop relationships with your customers

❑ Get the packaging right—pay attention to contextual issues

❑ Assess your image in the organization

❑ Decide what your image should be

❑ Plan, create, and promote the image you need

❑ Learn to maintain customer focus at all times

❑ Pay special attention to administration

The next five chapters will take you through these key areas. For each, you will find the rationale, some examples of good or neglected marketing techniques to demonstrate the effect of that area, an opportunity to reflect on what you are now doing, and some suggestions for what you can do on your own and with your team.

SUMMARY

This explanatory chapter moved towards a working definition of marketing, which is at the heart of this book. It also introduced implications of this definition for the training and development manager, as well as the scope of activities that you must attend to.

CHAPTER 3

How to Analyze Your Market

If we accept that ultimately marketing means getting the customer to WANT what you offer, then the implications are logical:

❑ You must know *who* your customers are

❑ You must know *what will satisfy* your customers

❑ You must communicate *how* you are matching your service to their need

WHO ARE YOUR CUSTOMERS?

One answer would be to say the entire organization is your customer. If the performance of each individual employee, whether part-time support staff or senior executive, counts, then each is your customer. However it is not useful to lump the entire organization into one customer base. You will have to focus different marketing approaches at different groups, so that the right messages are received.

While effective performance improvement strategy is, of course, linked to and driven by the business strategy, you cannot rely on the policy makers to include the training and development component in their communications on policy or business direction. To effectively provide the means of bridging the gap between what people are employed to do and what people are capable of doing, you must continually make the various customer groups aware of your role, your services, and your effectiveness in improving performance.

The first step is to consider the several broad categories that make up your customers:

❑ **Direct customers**—those that require training or development to perform effectively their job. These are the direct recipients of your efforts—the "participants." But while your job exists largely to provide them with development, focusing all your attention on them is insufficient. It is crucial to pay equal attention to the three other groups.

❑ **Sponsors**—Those people who hold the strings, whether purse strings or political strings. Without their support, you are skating on very thin ice indeed.

❑ **Influencers**—those who, through their power, prestige, or simply pervasiveness, can sway your direct customers and sponsors. They fall into several subcategories. *Champions* are the positive variety—those who will spread the good word and be your public relations volunteers whether officially (in newsletters or staff meetings) or informally (in the restaurant or on the train). Champions can come in many guises: beneficiaries of others' training, previous participants themselves who can influence others, secretaries or other direct reports of your sponsors, etc. *Blockers* and *doomsayers*—these are another variety of influencers who do you no good. Blockers are less vociferous than doomsayers, but where possible impede others from using or benefiting from your efforts. Doomsayers, as the name implies, are more active. For whatever reason, they work against you, stirring up negative feelings and turning people away. You must give blockers and doomsayers special attention either to neutralize their message or to turn them into champions.

❑ **Managers of your direct customers**—Perhaps they should be in a class with the influencers, but because of their unique positioning in relation to your direct customers, there are particular considerations which makes separating them useful.

The Direct Customers

Potentially, this group encompasses everyone in the organization. However, by identifying discrete groups, you will be able to focus your communication and services in a more appropriate, targeted manner. You have organization charts, results of annual appraisals, various management reports, "grapevine" information, and your knowledge of the corporate direction and strategy. You may have done a formal needs analysis; certainly you have done informal ones. From these or other sources, you should be able to identify customer "groups." Some will be all or part of particular departments (e.g., site engineers or customer service representatives); others will be a slice of the whole organization (e.g., female supervisors, mid-level managers, department heads). You will most likely find both kinds of groupings.

The first step is to identify who they are, specifically, for your organization. One useful technique for doing this is to "map" them, mind-map fashion, on a white board or a sheet of flipchart paper. (Mind-map is a trade-marked term invented by Tony Buzan. See Further Reading.) If you can do this activity with one or more staff members, you are less likely to forget any of the relevant groups. Figure 3.1 illustrates a customer map.

Once you establish different customer groups within the organization, as with any other product or service, effective marketing

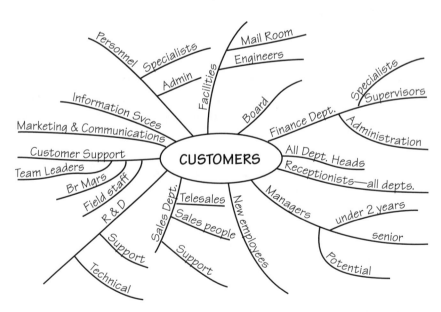

Figure 3-1. A customer map.

requires that you differentiate between them; in that way the relevance of what you are providing—to *"me"* and *"my* job"—will be apparent to the target group.

The customer map will serve as a template that you can return to time and time again, whenever a performance need arises. It will further enable you to see links between customer groups that otherwise may easily escape you.

Case in Point

The training department in a manufacturing company was approached by a team of credit department managers, who requested that the training department "do something" for the department's operational staff. The operational staff had been undergoing severe cutbacks and was suffering from extremely low morale resulting in lagging performance and reluctance to take on further responsibility. Management determined that the staff needed to feel more confident in their own abilities so they could make decisions and communicate more assertively with clients. The particular staff were young, had little higher education, were rather unsophisticated, and had not been used to being expected to think for themselves. The trainers designed a workshop specifically for them. It was very successful and produced positive effects for the entire operational staff.

The training manager realized that there was another group in the order department, which was in a similar situation as the credit department's operational staff. The training manager demonstrated the links between the problems that the order department was experiencing and the outcomes of the workshops that the credit group attended. As a result, the training manager instituted a very similar workshop as a regular development activity for all one-year staff.

The Sponsors

You can find power sources in organizations in many places. Surely your boss or your boss's boss is one you need to be aware of, but there are many others. To identify your sponsors, ask yourself the following questions:

❑ Who can "pull the plug" on various department initiatives?
❑ Who can re-allocate essential funds?

❑ Who in the organization is most often quoted in the press?

❑ Whose words make people who are more senior than you "jump?"

❑ Is there an heir (heiress) apparent? a favored "next in line?"

You may not like answering the previous questions but you ignore this information at your peril.

If you have an organization chart, look at it closely and *think* about the names that fill the boxes. Remember that power does not always come from the higher level. What are the personalities? What have various individuals caused to happen (or not happen) during the past year? Who has lunch with whom? Who carpools together? Who sees each other socially? Who has a long history working for or with the figureheads, perhaps in previous organizations?

Lest this imply too much arbitrary use of power, you can look for sponsors in a more positive way. Consider the real drivers of the business. Is it the CEO, particular members of senior management, the finance director, etc.?

❑ Who, through charisma or sound business vision, possibly both, keeps your organization moving forward from the top?

❑ At what strategic goal is a particular training activity aimed?

❑ Who expresses the most concern about performance improvement activities?

❑ How much does senior management really know about what you are doing as a training and development department to make their corporate vision possible?

Identify the key players that you must consistently influence to maintain your own power. (An often neglected entry to this level is the "influencer" group made up of the secretaries. Treat these gatekeepers with respect and acknowledge their influence. Discuss your intentions with them so that they are aware of how your plans fit with their bosses' interests. You may also learn a lot!) It is vital to ensure that your employee performance improvement strategy is *seen* to be an essential part of the business strategy. You will have to focus some of your marketing efforts in this direction as well as at your direct customers, to ensure that these sponsors feel your efforts are adding value to what *they* determine is important.

Do this well and you will have a mighty safety net. Let it slip, and regardless of the demonstrated results of your efforts, you can be subject to what may look like arbitrary withdrawal of support.

Case in Point

A well-known communications company responded to an expressed need for improving internal promotability. They designed a development center, which assessed core competencies that the broader organization needed. Managers were encouraged to apply so they could build a career development plan that went beyond their current functional area. Their managers were encouraged to support the development center (by allowing participation) as it would contribute to the greater good of the organization.

Industrial psychologists who were engaged for the purpose carefully designed the day. It included relevant psychometric testing, exercises drawn from their observations inside the organization, a feedback component, and an offer for follow-up counseling on a one-to-one basis to help the individual design an appropriate career development plan.

The psychologists trained observers from inside the company and piloted the event. The first time it ran, nine managers attended and all of them reported positively on the experience. They felt it helped them see possibilities within the organization and learned what they had to do to make the possibilities a reality.

The company's training department ran the development center two more times during the first year. Then they convened all involved (participants and developers) to review its success. Two managers who had attended the very first event had been promoted, and three were engaged in specific development activities targeted to their own needs. Everyone involved thought the development center was a great success because it met its objectives of providing the organization with internal candidates for promotional opportunities.

Unfortunately, assessment and development centers are expensive to design and run, due to the concentration of personnel needed for each one and the limited number of candidates that can attend at any one time.

Despite the achievement of the development center's objectives and the investment in time and money that went into its creation, senior management eliminated the development center 20 months later as part of a cost-cutting activity.

The Influencers: Champions, Blockers, and Doomsayers

Having the internal grapevine spread the word on your behalf can be a key contributor to your ongoing success. You want people to frequently hear positive things about what you are doing. Influencers operate whether we like it or not, so it is far better to identify them and build on the positive, ones who will champion your efforts. There may also be potential champions among the "silent ones"— blockers who one way or another keep the message from spreading. Finally, determine if you have doomsayers spreading any kind of negative information.

Who are the particular influencers of your direct customers? Certainly all those who experience direct benefits from your customers' training—their managers, their colleagues in other departments, their suppliers, their own customers. If your organization has a mentoring system, mentors will have tremendous influence on your direct customers—all these are potential "champions" if you make sure they recognize the benefits.

You can find other influencers by considering who the most influential groups are within your organization. What about official "PR"? Do people read the company newsletter? Does the newsletter carry any weight? Other useful questions to help you discover pockets of influence: What are new and prospective employees told about training and development opportunities? Do your recruitment people know what training and development activities new employees may experience? And just how good are these activities? How can you ensure the recruiters deliver the right message? This kind of "grassroots" marketing is just as important as focusing on your direct customer and sponsors.

It doesn't mean you'll be trying to sell water wings to a duck. You're still designing solutions to meet real business needs of particular groups within your organization. However, within those groups, there will be many who weren't in on (or don't remember) the needs analysis, who don't have a manager who will brief them on the value, necessity, and expected outcomes of the training. These people need to be influenced from other sources. If one of their colleagues casually discusses the benefits of a recent training activity to his/her job, your "target customer" may well be encouraged to pursue your training service for him or herself.

Activity

1. Consider some recent training you were involved in and list what positive and negative messages participants might have received about the event prior to attending.

Positive message	Negative message
_____	_____
_____	_____
_____	_____
_____	_____

2. Attribute each of the above messages to a specific source.

Message	Source
_____	_____
_____	_____
_____	_____
_____	_____

3. Label each source from number 2 as either a champion, blocker, or doomsayer

Source	Influencer
_____	_____
_____	_____
_____	_____
_____	_____

4. For each influencer, indicate the amount of influence (power) you perceive him/her to wield in the organization by assigning a number 1–5. One is least influence, five is most influence.

Influencer	(1–5)
_____	_____
_____	_____
_____	_____
_____	_____

Line Managers of Direct Customers

An essential group of influencers are the line managers of your direct customers. While successful training and development professionals know they should always involve the line management in their own staff's training, they may have not considered it as a marketing technique. Good management briefing, however, which creates partnership and ownership of the solution, resulting in interest and reinforcement back on the job, is certainly the best "support" marketing you can do.

The following case is an example of how the benefits that followed one training activity went beyond the initial population and generated interest from other groups who could derive the same benefit.

Case in Point

A large public-sector organization determined that its newly merged communications department needed improved teamworking. The previously separate teams had provided similar services in the past and had to re-allocate its work in a way that enhanced cooperation among the team members. There was a further objective to develop a more customer-oriented approach to the rest of the organization. Following a successful series of team-building events, several of the "users" of the communications department became aware of improved service.

The training manager, who made it her business to mingle with line management and listen to their comments, capitalized on this awareness by interviewing some of the recipients of the improved service and having an article published (by the communications department) in the in-house newsletter. The article referred to the team-building events that led to the changed performance.

The resulting requests for similar training came from several other service departments.

SETTING PRIORITIES

We have established that to satisfy your customers, it is necessary to identify all customer groups and provide appropriate solutions for each one. However, it is rare that all groups will have their performance needs met equally. If you are part of a large organization, there are perhaps dedicated professionals responsible for training and development for particular departments, although even so, funds and expertise will certainly not be unlimited. In the smaller concerns, you will certainly have to make some tough decisions as to where to focus your energy, as you will not always be able to respond to all of your customers.

Trying to do it all—be all things to all people—will only result in a half-baked end product. You will need a method of deciding where to focus your resources at any particular time. It's not a good idea to fall into the trap of "oiling the squeakiest wheel." It's much more political, not to mention strategical, to scan the organization and make a rational decision that you can justify.

There are different ways to approach this problem. Three are outlined below.

The Biggest Payoff

To remain a market-led function, the strategic training and development manager should consider where the biggest payoffs will come from when determining the bulk of training solutions to be undertaken. A payoff is more than the expected results of the training activity. It includes the benefits of those results in the wider context of the organization. And in some cases, the payoff may simply be pleasing a powerful backer or loyal influencer.

Payoffs might be the effects of the learning experience on the section or department that took part in the training, for instance decreases in processing time and service complaints. They may be organizational payoffs that are not immediately visible to the participant group, for example, improved recruitment techniques saving huge amounts in hiring costs, or increased numbers of contracts following training in relationship-selling skills.

One way to look at payoffs is to view the possibilities against very specific criteria—for example, *relevance, awareness,* and *added value:*

1. First, consider how relevant your suggestions are to solving the performance or organizational problem. If your ideas are weak at this point, reconsider.

2. Next, think how aware your customer groups might be of the subject areas of your proposals. If their current awareness is low, and relevance is high, you can expect them to be surprised.

3. Finally, consider how much added value the training or development solution will generate—again, if it is high, you are more likely to create an impact.

You might already have worked out that—from a marketing point of view—the proposals with greatest impact have low current awareness (high surprise value) and high added value (a strong payoff). There are good reasons for this. Proposals that carry high awareness and high added value have probably already been identified, and may already be scheduled. Those with high awareness and low added value look relatively unattractive, while those with low awareness and low added value might be risky, if you raise awareness and it doesn't pay off. Figure 3-2 illustrates this concept. The next step is to start looking at a range of specific options and allocate weightings for the criteria that are consistent with the view your organization takes.

This reasoning may not apply absolutely if you operate a monopoly, but it is a useful starting point for first guessing how your customers, sponsors, and influencers may react. Once you reach this point, you can start looking more closely at specific payoffs.

Certainly if you can demonstrate significant performance improvement, revenue increases, complaint reduction, and the like, you have a valuable payoff. The payoff may, however, come in the form of kudos from senior management ("What a change!" or "I didn't think you

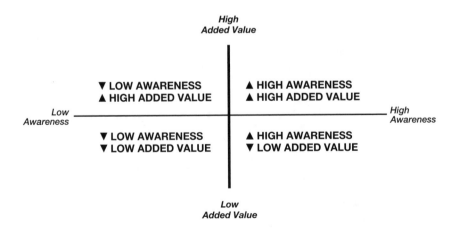

Figure 3-2. Model for assessing training payoffs.

could do it—more, please!") It might be in the form of enhanced public relations—press coverage, for example, which may be used to promote the business. It's not uncommon for companies to boast about
their customer service training in their print or television advertising.

The Internal Payoff

Questions to ask when looking for payoffs

❏ *Benefit questions:*

How much money will it save/bring in?

Who will it please—besides the participants? Why? Why is that
important?

What would happen if it weren't done? (Be specific)

❏ *Cost considerations:*

How much money will it cost? Does it require external
resources, extensive research or planning time?

Does it require involvement of large numbers of people? Can
you get their cooperation easily?

How long will it take for the results to be noticed?

There is no easy solution for identifying payoffs, but answering these
questions will help you make reasonable decisions as to what you can
successfully accomplish.

Perhaps a part of your organization approaches you to support a
training program that will absorb too much of your budget. Using the
techniques described, can you amass sufficient evidence of high added
value to justify support for special funding? Can you also target
potential sponsors, whose awareness of the project will be low, to
benefit from raising awareness?

You can also develop a cost/benefit chart, called here a payoff
matrix (see Figure 3-3)—with an added category, time—to help you
see what you have to work with. Use whatever subcategories make
sense in your own situation.

The payoff matrix looks time-consuming. Until you are familiar
with this type of analysis and you have developed processes with

	BENEFIT				COST				TIME
	Money saved/ gained	Recipient delight	Consequence if not done	Block time away from job	External Consult	Documentation	Development time	Staffing	to take effect
Cust. Care (staff)	H	H	H	L	H	H	VH	VH	1 yr
Cust. Care (mgmt)	H	H	H	M	L	M	M	M	1 yr
Perf. Mgmt	L	H	M	M	—	—	M	L	6 mos
Recr. interv'g	M	VH	M	H	—	—	L	M	1 yr
Supv. Skls Review	L	M	L	L	—	—	L	L	6 mos

Figure 3-3. An example of a payoff matrix.

which you feel comfortable, you are likely to be on a steep learning curve. But there is an additional payoff, if you get it right—you will have powerful tools for convincing your potential sponsors to back a particular program.

In Figure 3-3, the training manager assigned specific boundaries to very high (VH), high (H), medium (M), and (L) low. For example, under "recipient delight," VH (very high) means both sponsors and direct customers are particularly keen to have this training; whereas, H (high) means sponsors see it as essential but direct customers do not (perhaps because they think they already possess the skills involved). This latter situation will require some very well-targeted marketing strategies to get your customer to want your service.

It's up to you to define your criteria and the parameters of whatever indicators you use. You may, for example, want to include risks: "Risks of not training" and "Risks of failure." A sense of your own organizational climate will help you determine the right categories. But you don't have to do it alone. Working through a matrix of this type is an excellent team-building activity for one of your own team meetings; or, if you have no staff, perhaps your boss or a group of manager/customers can share in the analysis.

Your task will be to make sure that the payoff is acknowledged by a wide spectrum of organizational VIPs (your sponsors) and those whose word is listened to (don't forget the external customer)—that's where visibility enters the picture. Some training results are immediately visible; most are not. Part of your job is to help make those payoffs visible. (See previous case example. We'll spend more time on this in Chapter 7.)

Build a Critical Mass

If you want to demonstrate the effectiveness of your endeavors to the larger organization, and there is some doubt among the staff at large, you will find it useful to analyze your customers in another way: according to their levels of trust in you and agreement with your purpose. An international consultant who specializes in managing change contributed Figure 3-4.

The key here is to identify into which area particular customers fall. You will then know where to start. Your high-value customers are on the right-hand side—the allies for obvious reasons, but also the opponents. Because of the trust that exists between you, they will

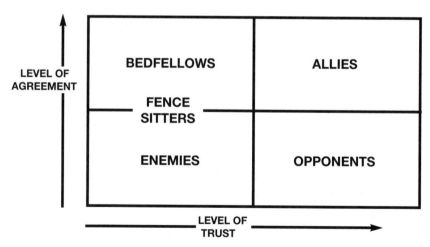

Figure 3-4. Customer differentiation. (From Managing the Dynamics of Change, Vic Hall, Paris.)

work very hard to see things from your viewpoint. As these groups begin showing the effects of your efforts, the line in the middle will move to the left.

Finally, it is not totally inappropriate to consider the strengths and development needs of the training department in determining which projects to address. For example, to test and develop the skills of your newest training officer, you may consider assigning a revamp of the staff orientation course. And certainly, after developing good relationships with your influencers and sponsors, you will want to meet *their* needs as much as possible, even if they are not high on the business strategy agenda.

So while not all you do will be a result of your "payoff matrix," it would be prudent to keep tabs on the balance of your efforts and make sure you're seen to be serving the right customers in the right way.

ACTIVITY

1. Create a customer map showing all the possible customer groupings you must serve (see Figure 3-1 on page 28).

2. Identify the sponsors and influencers in each case.

    Sponsors   **Influencers**

    _____   _____

    _____   _____

    _____   _____

    _____   _____

3. Complete a payoff matrix for two or three possible initiatives you are coordinating (see Figure 3-3 on page 38).

SUMMARY

This chapter focused on the customers that make up your market. We discussed why it is vital to identify at least three different customer groupings and in what ways you can vary your marketing approach to meet the different needs of each group. This chapter also introduced methods of "segmenting" your customer base.

Lastly, we looked at a way to determine how to allocate your resources so that the right customers benefit and you are seen to be both a strategic and a successful part of your organization.

CHAPTER 4

Building Relationships: Customers Are People Too

So far, our discussion about customer groups may have seemed mechanistic or even instrumental. Focusing on analyzing, segmenting, targeting, and prioritizing your customers does detract from the fact that customers are indeed people. As people, your relationships with them are crucial to accomplishing any of the preceding activities and those that follow. In addition, forming relationships will provide you with many obvious and less obvious benefits.

When concentrating on performance improvement for a large population, or working on a project for one particular group, it is easy for your attention to slip from the relationship building that must continue with individuals not connected with the current effort. For sustainability, it is essential that you build and nurture these relationships. Priorities can change quickly in organizations, sometimes with very limited notice. To have or rapidly gain entry to a group who could benefit from your partnership, it is enormously helpful to have an existing relationship.

Despite the fact that Human Resources professionals tend to be "people persons," current projects commonly get in the way of the people contacts that you need to maintain. It is easy to get caught up in the task—in the business at hand. One of the classic tensions in organizations is getting the balance right between the people and the task focus [1]. A people focus is nonetheless crucial; to paraphrase Jim Cathcart, author of *Relationship Selling* [2],

"Poor human relations can ruin the best marketing efforts."

What this means in the current context is that the training and development team must possess or develop excellent relationship skills. They must make a concerted effort to form, develop, and nurture relationships with a wide range of individuals within the organization.

Different relationships involve different levels of attention and service. An analogy here would be to consider the friends and acquaintances you have. Some of them you are quite happy to see occasionally, perhaps because there is only minimal common interest. You occasionally attend the theater together, or have a meal. You don't feel slighted if you don't hear from them for a month or two. There are other people you "have a lot of time for," because both you and they derive significant personal satisfaction from the contact. These people can drop in on you or be called at the last minute with a spontaneous plan. You send each other postcards when you are on vacation, notice things the other would like when shopping, etc. You know what they're up to, how they feel, what their needs are. You expect them to keep you informed of changes in their lives. This same range of requirements and responses applies to organizational relationships.

If you can evaluate your customer relationships in terms of the level of service that is required, you will be able to "schedule" the amount of attention you need to give and plan the time and resources necessary to service this need more appropriately.

HOW A CUSTOMER RELATIONSHIP DEVELOPS

There is a logical progression in the development of a relationship between supplier and customer. Figure 4-1 depicts this progression graphically.

Stage I extends from the first meeting to the initial provision of some service. Between these two points, a building of understanding occurs on each side. This is usually accomplished by asking questions to understand the context in which the individual or team operates as well as by sharing information about yourself and how you and/or

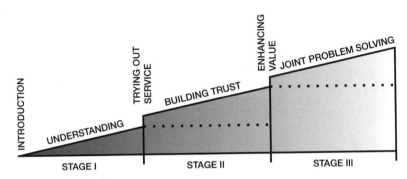

Figure 4-1. Stages in customer relationships.

your function works. Ideally, Stage 1 is a face-to-face stage, beginning before there is a known problem to solve. It can, however, be condensed to a telephone conversation, provided that you employ excellent listening and questioning skills.

At a certain point the nature of the customer's problem will become sufficiently clear to you and you will be ready to offer a solution. This is when you may be poised for Stage II. Whether you get there or not will depend on the willingness and ability of each of you to build a deeper level of trust. There are many ways this can occur, for example

❑ Showing vulnerabilities, e.g., the customer admits feelings of insecurity or incompetence

❑ Allowing experimentation, e.g., you reach an agreement to pilot a previously unproven solution

❑ Admitting mistakes and errors of judgment, e.g., the training manager acknowledges the wrong approach was chosen—and immediately moves to correct the situation

Continuing to focus on the relationship at this point, through demonstration of commitment to customer satisfaction, will deepen the relationship as well as enhance the value of the solution. It will allow the beginnings of a closer alliance, thereby creating what an East Coast consulting group [3] calls a "key relationship" customer. Alternatively, if either party causes the key focus to be simply the delivery of the promised solution (a focus on the product), the relationship can plateau at Stage 1. In the framework that follows, this is referred to as a "transactional customer."

Moving from Stage II to Stage III involves a further deepening of the relationship into a sense of full partnership. Again, there can be plateauing at Stage II. Key relationship customers may stay just that or, at some point, develop into fuller, richer partnerships. The ongoing nurturing of the relationship will greatly affect its future.

An example of a Stage II relationship comes from a global banking organization. Acting in the performance consulting model described in Chapter 1, the learning consultant is made aware of a problem in a retail outlet in another state where tellers are not balancing their cash drawers. Not having a prior relationship with this particular business unit, the learning consultant must move quickly into Stage II in order to demonstrate a viable service. A telephone discussion served as the Stage I introduction, following which the learning consultant compiled some thought-provoking questions (a quick diagnostic tool), which he faxed to the customer. The resulting answers made it possible for him to draw up a performance contract. The learning consultant then met with the tellers and helped them brainstorm the barriers they perceived—it was not a training issue. This meeting led to a solution in which they agreed upon a way ahead. They then set about developing mechanisms to overcome the barriers. The learning consultant then returned to base, with communication mechanisms in place to gather success stories and any problems from the customer group. The effort was a success and, with no further contact until a new problem comes up, will remain a Stage II relationship.

Stage III, engaging in joint problem-solving and together formulating the solutions, produces a partnering relationship. Like any true partnership, full trust and respect, openness and sharing values are the cornerstones. Stage III relationships are the most fulfilling and give the highest level of support within the organization. In the previous example, if there was interest, time, and perceived benefit on both sides, the consultant and the customer could have continued developing their relationship to learn from each other—with mutual benefit—as time went on. You should note that it is not possible, and would indeed not be reasonable to have Stage III relationships as the aim of all customer interactions. The following summarizes the nature of each type of relationship and the level of attention required.

Types of Relationships	Relationship Requirements
Transactional Customers: those clients who opt for the "plain vanilla" training products, with little or no customization. They call on you as needed and are mostly interested in existing off-the-shelf solutions.	Maintain ongoing, but infrequent contact. Most contact will remain at the product and implementation levels.
Key Relationship Customers: those clients for whom you are the primary supplier of custom-developed programs and ongoing consultant interventions; together you strive to build understanding, trust, and respect beyond the immediate project.	Nurture these customers by looking for opportunities to support their goals, and to enhance the relationship towards partnering.
Partnering Customers: those clients with the following characteristics: ❑ Long-term commitment—three to five years or more. ❑ Consultative business focus—centered on identifying and solving important customer problems and maximizing customer opportunities based on understanding the customer's situation, not just selling services or products. ❑ Shared values and interests—committed to high levels of openness, truth, and support and to establishing a high level of trust, an open sharing of values and goals, mutual disclosure, discourse, and discovery.	There are a variety of connecting points between your function and the customer organization with a blurring of the lines in between. A joint commitment exists to develop and maintain deep relationships to innovatively solve problems together.

Central to the categorization of customer relationships are the ideas that

❑ you are responsible for the relationship

❑ you accept different objectives for the relationship and expend different levels of energy for each group

❑ you plan contact that is intended to strengthen the relationship

Forming, developing, and nurturing relationships involve both skills and systems. The personal skills of relationships are widely documented, and are no doubt the subject of many books in the reader's library. They include an ability to empathize and take certain risks to develop trust, and the ability to influence. A review of both the Johari Window [4] and any good influencing-skills model will be useful here. It is of course possible that review will not be enough, and that the competence in relationship skills will need developing. It might be wise to devote a team meeting to some form of assessment of the relationship skills and, if necessary, plan a skills-development strategy.

It is not enough, however, just to have good relationship skills. Methods for "connecting" and a system for keeping in touch are also essential.

Case In Point

Sophie, the head of organization development at an established retail chain, knew from various signs within the organization, her professional reading, her association with colleagues in different companies, and perhaps her sixth sense that the company had to make some major culture shifts if it was to survive. This was not, however, a message she could deliver at a senior management meeting. There were issues of her own credibility around business issues (she was hired to run training) as well as the fact that she had not actually developed any relationships with the movers and shakers. (Her efforts to have periodic, brief one-to-one meetings were frequently thwarted by the managers' last minute schedule changes.) She was frustrated both at not being able to act on her professional concerns and at not being allowed entry into the power circles where she could make her case.

Sophie came upon a successful plan to establish both a relationship and her credibility with the managers. A frequent user of the Internet for research, she often downloaded articles of professional interest from a range of international business sites. She began to sort through them and pulled out those that highlighted organizations which had achieved the types of culture shifts she thought were necessary and other relevant topics that were probably not on the senior managers' reading list. She sent copies of various articles to individuals on the senior management team, each with a handwritten note as to how interesting she found it and why she thought it relevant.

Within a few months she found her "one-to-one's" began to happen, and there was now a useful topic for discussion as well. Relationship establishment had begun and she is certain that it was instrumental in her being asked to arrange and facilitate a senior management retreat to review and plan the long-term goals of the organization.

Other methods of gaining access to customers include inviting them to comment on some current or future organizational endeavor, either in focus groups or asking for one-to-one meetings [5].

KEEPING IN TOUCH

You can keep in touch with people in various ways, ranging from weekly or monthly meetings to monthly reviews of a contact database, followed by a few telephone calls. The point is that there should be a system. It should not be left to chance.

Case In Point

Jonathan is the group manager of management development for a world-renowned service company that has offices around the globe. One of the functions of the management development group is to run key programs that both update the participants with new information and fuel them with the appropriate skills so they can move up in the organization. The programs are limited to approximately 500 people each year, while the organization has about 25,000 potential participants.

Routinely, at divisional meetings, Jonathan's office delivers the training schedule so that the divisional vice presidents, representing the largest countries—those providing the biggest return for the company—can select who will attend. Therefore the offices in the smaller countries or areas with low returns get the information last and by that time there are either only a few available spots in the program or none at all.

In terms of a standard payoff matrix (see Chapter 3), this official process makes sense. Jonathan, however, was concerned that high-potential individuals from the smaller countries were missing out completely and would therefore never be poised for advancement. So Jonathan began an unofficial routine in parallel with the official one.

Whenever a divisional training program announcement is to be made, Jonathan makes a personal telephone call to the managers of the offices located in the smaller countries to advise them of the up-and-coming program, inviting them to select appropriate individuals to attend. Because of the personal contact, Jonathan is able to balance the needs of both groups making sure that needs of major players are met while still accommodating some of the managers from the smaller locations.

While the benefit to the client company is that it gets the opportunity to develop future managers, the management development function (Jonathan), receives the benefit of becoming a trusted professional by the client company. Now when there is a need for some training intervention he is already in the Stage II level.

A recent example of how this approach paid off was when the small, underused office in China suddenly found itself as part of a country making giant leaps into western economic markets. Jonathan was quickly able to work with the managers there and began planning how to develop performance to meet the new and constantly growing needs.

ADDED VALUE

In addition to the obvious marketing edge widespread customer relationships provide, there are other benefits for the training and development professional. Customer relationships offer a unique approach to understanding functional areas. Often HR professionals have no hands-on experience in the business, or else come from one particular functional area. Customer relationships can give the professional an operational perspective on the business and sometimes the industry as a whole. By getting immersed into other functional areas through developing relationships with a cross section of people, functional credibility and possibly broader career prospects can ensue. And finally, it is not unusual for sound social relationships to develop out of the customer-supplier familiarity.

SUMMARY

This chapter highlighted the people side of the customer-supplier equation, explaining the value of developing relationships with prospective as well as current customers. We presented a model of the customer relationship stages along with a method for categorizing different relationships according to the type of involvement desired, and therefore, a way to allocate time. Finally, we discussed methods of gaining access and of keeping in touch.

REFERENCES/NOTES

1. For a comprehensive discussion on balancing opposite forces within organizations, read Barry Johnson, Ph.D., *Polarity Management,* 1992, HRD Press, MA.

2. Jim Cathcart, *Relationship Selling: The Key to Getting and Keeping Customers,* 1990, Perigree Books, NY.

3. Suggestions for the customer relationship categories and the description of the type and level of attention are used with permission from Harvey Lifton and Michael Lynch of New Jersey, who find this framework of relationship categories useful in allocating resources to their clients.

4. Developed by Joseph Luft and Harry Ingham. See Joseph Luft, *Of Human Interaction,* 1969, Palo Alto, CA, National Press Books, or as described and annotated for managers' interactions, by Jay Hall in *Models for Management: The Structure of Competence,* 1988, Woodstead Press.

5. A good example of using focus groups to develop partnership can be found "Hardwiring the Learning Organization," *Training and Development,* ASTD, August 1997.

CHAPTER 5

Getting the Packaging Right

Raising your awareness of contextual areas will give you some ideas for fine-tuning them to match the needs and perceptions of your customers.

BEYOND CONTENT—MATCHING CONTEXT TO CULTURE

In the past ten years or so HRD has moved much closer to organizational strategy. Increased academic rigor in the U.S. and higher levels of professional qualifications for trainers in other countries have had a positive effect for the discipline of training and development itself. Training and development practitioners, however, still tend to act closely to what they perceive as professional guidelines. In *The Theory and Practice of Training*, Buckley and Caple (1992) point out that trainers must become more sensitive to what works best for managers at the "sharp end" rather than concentrate on what is best for trainers and what always has been done in the past. Looking at context means going beyond what might have been known as the best way to generate a useful learning experience and focusing on issues of format, timing, environment, and personal style.

Format

While assessing a perceived training need often throws up a non-training solution, that solution may still come under the auspices of

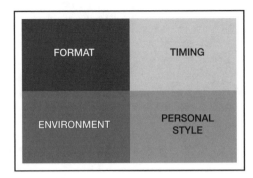

Figure 5-1. Context issues.

the training and development function. Format refers to how the improved performance gets delivered—it encompasses all the various training delivery alternatives, including guided self-development, group activities, one-to-one arrangements, etc. Concern for format requires you to start with a blank slate when recommending a solution, then to create a format that suits the particular customer group, the organization at large, and possibly the individual.

Case in Point

Recently the training department of a large service organization launched a well-researched and professionally designed series of performance appraisal workshops. The impetus came from the top; as part of the strategy to enable the firm to continue competing successfully in the future, the organization was to install a performance management system. As a key element in the system, all who had management responsibilities had to conduct performance appraisals with all who reported to them. Then the training department announced the impending workshops. The training staff consulted with line managers, seeking their input on how the system would operate and how training should be handled. All agreed that this was what "they" needed. Unfortunately, "they" was just that—the other guy. The workshops were well received by supervisory and first level management, but more-senior managers found excuse after excuse for not attending. After several months of puzzlement, the training staff finally understood that the higher level people thought the training (which they had helped to design) was somehow "beneath them." Several mentioned they could read the material and proceed with the system on their own. The training manager was certain that many needed to work on their interpersonal skills, and that unsupervised reading would not build their skills in this area.

Through hindsight, the training manager realized that she should have pitched the training differently to those at different levels in the organization. Perhaps she could have distributed materials and then held a briefing meeting for senior managers—using the same materials and activities as in the training course. The objective was to get managers at all levels to use the system effectively, not to get them all into training workshops. The same content needed to be disseminated; the context, in this case the format, needed to be quite different, to preserve the ego needs of senior management in a culture where vulnerability posed a perceived threat.

A particular need in the previous case was for the more senior people to feel they were getting *appropriate* treatment. They certainly didn't want their juniors around when they floundered in a role-play exercise. And their particular status consciousness meant that their roles were highlighted as different from those they managed. Even though the procedures (and the resistance, fear, and trepidation) were quite similar between the more senior and the lower level managers, the format should have demonstrated that their training was in fact tailor-made for them. The training manager in question thought later that she should have involved the senior managers in *facilitating* the program. Their own training would have then been in the guise of "train-the-trainer" and seen as a higher responsibility than that of their trainees.

Format options for training are extensive; consider the following:

❏ Plan a series of short meetings (evenings, lunchtime, weekly breakfast sessions, etc.) and call them something else (executive briefings, management seminars, problem clinics)—the possibilities are limitless

❏ Have workbook and facilitated discussion sessions

❏ Develop or buy technology-based packages

❏ Incorporate a short module into a larger course

❏ Offer one-on-one mentoring systems

❏ Co-opt staff or managers for short-term training assignments

❏ Use line managers to train staff

❏ Use peer review groups

❏ Observe participants in the workplace and provide follow-up coaching

❏ Have the would-be participants design training modules—and run them on each other

❏ Include same-level attendees vs. multi-level attendees (horizontal vs. vertical "slicing")

❏ Have intact work teams vs. people who don't know each other

❏ Offer outdoor vs. classroom training

❏ Plan business simulation or experiential event vs. lecture-based presentation

Only your imagination will limit your format options. The key is to be sensitive to the customer and forget "what we've always done."

A few years ago, it became popular to "put everyone through" a customer-care awareness event. The rationale was that everyone would get the same message and see others getting it as well. However, ask any "vertical slice" of an organization who has done such an exercise and you'll find quite different reactions to the experience—many of them negative: "Too busy to be here," "Not relevant to me," "Great fun—but why?" and so on. Often, more-senior people attend out of duty or "orders" and do not accept that they need to hear the message. They are not, in fact, committed to "learning mode." If you change the training format to one in which they learn the principles, but also have an opportunity to look at them in the context of their own responsibilities, you will notice that the training will have much more impact. For example, involving them in the training can have a significant impact on the outcome.

Most companies have annual business conferences, often promoting the theme for the year—everyone is forced to attend; the hours are long; the benefit is miniscule. Trying to think "outside the box," Chris Turner, the "Learning Person" at the billion-dollar global company, Xerox Business Systems, decided to stage a very different kind of event to kickstart a culture change to become a "learning organization." The following description of the event appeared in a national magazine:

> We staged a Worldwide Learning Conference in 1995, kind of a "learning Woodstock" . . . The vision was to create an event for a few days that would let people experience a learning organization—what it feels like, and how much fun it can be . . . Picture this: you walk into the hotel on the first day, and

instead of the usual corporate meeting there's a huge ballroom with globes and stars and moons hanging from the ceiling, music from all over the world playing, life-size cardboard cutouts. It immediately says to people: This is different.

There was no individual recognition, no speeches by corporate officers. We had outside speakers, simulations, seminars. Then at the end of the first day, we opened Xpo, with more than two dozen booths displaying all the different kinds of XBS tools and applications. We even had a booth where we sold "learning clothes"—items with our change strategy logo and graphics—and we ended up selling $90,000 worth in just two days. We were afraid nobody would want to go to Xpo, that they'd just want to go play golf. We couldn't get them to leave!

The four-and-a-half days became a metaphor for forever: "Would you like to feel this way after every day of work? Let us help you! It can be this way all the time!" [1]

ACTIVITY

1. Look back on your training output for the past year. Make a short list of the different kinds of events you ran or oversaw, and the percentage of each.

Events	Percentage
_____	_____
_____	_____
_____	_____
_____	_____
_____	_____

2. Did any customer groups respond particularly positively or negatively to your formats?

_____

_____

_____

_____

_____

3. Are any useful formats missing?

_____

_____

_____

_____

4. Who attended each kind of event (vertical slices, departments, mixed groups, complete teams, etc.)?

_____

_____

_____

_____

5. What alternatives are your currently considering for different customer groups?

_____

_____

_____

_____

Program names and job titles

While we are dealing with the issue of format, let's also discuss briefly how you label what you do. Course titles can be business-oriented: "Achieving Results Through People" or "The Winning Negotiator"; intriguing: "I'm OK—How Are You?" or "Inventing Your Future"; functional: "Time and Priority Management" or "Communication Skills"; active: "Leadership in Action" or "Helping the Customer."

The choice lies with you and your sponsor, but be aware that the way in which you label your initiatives and materials carries important messages. Labeling is a vital promotional tool. You do need to consider your cultural environment, but also think about the messages course titles convey.

One financial service organization increased registration by 100 percent when they changed the training course title from "Presentation Skills" to "Persuasive Presentations."

If your culture demands descriptive labels, you can always consider using sub-titles or sub-headings. The same applies to job titles. Are your staff known as trainers, tutors, instructors, consultants, advisors, learning specialists, or something else? Are you the manager of training, training and development, human resource development, education, learning and development, or another term? Not all these things may be yours to decide, but if you form a clear idea of what you want to project to your chosen marketplaces, you will have a much better idea of what to ask for and promote—and your reasons for doing so—when you are dealing with your directors and sponsors.

Timing

Some large organizations have moved to "just in time" training—bringing the needed training to the individual just at the time the learning is needed, often in the form of self-paced technology-based learning rather than group activity. However, courses and training programs have certainly not disappeared. What has changed is the acceptance of past procedures. The long three-day course in a 2,000-person company is not accepted in today's lean organizations. There are simply not enough people left to keep the work going. Many companies perceive the traditional training day as an unrealistic luxury, especially if it demands that several people from one work area attend. Many organizations have even curtailed short early-morning training activities.

Part of looking at training needs involves finding out when the would-be participants can actually take part and adjusting formats creatively to match the business priorities. Many four-week residential management courses have already given way to shorter and modular approaches. But alternatives don't stop at 9 to 5 on weekdays. A series of weekend, evening, early morning, or midday working lunch sessions can be very acceptable ways to provide training sessions—especially if the environment is congenial. One investment bank found that running two 4 p.m.–7 p.m. sessions a week worked best.

Those times might be awkward for the trainer, but most can be persuaded by the benefits, and there are undoubtedly some who would thrive on these "odd" hours. All of this is consistent with what we know about the modern workforce, which less frequently expects traditional ways of doing things, and expects instead more pragmatic, previously unorthodox solutions.

Timing also means being sensitive to customers' important deadlines and heavy work periods. At the simplest level, it means that you should find out if certain days of the week are better than others for scheduling training. At a more complex level: When do appraisals take place? When is the corporate year-end? Is there a seasonal pattern of activity? What events impact the workload?

Another aspect of timing is use of time during the training program itself. Sometimes you should include long breaks to promote discussion or completion of an activity; sometimes activities are assigned to be completed during lunch breaks or between training days. Adhering to past procedures: "We always allow 15 minutes for coffee," "Lunch is from 1 p.m. to 2 p.m." can be artificial and needless constraints. Consider the group's "time" needs. Useful questions to ask yourself about the training group in question are

❑ Is the training group used to quick decisions and fast-paced action (will they buckle under time pressures)?

❑ Will they need time to call the office and deal with emergencies or risk "tuning out" for the rest of the day?

❑ Will their culture (both ethnic or organizational) set time expectations which have to be acknowledged?

❑ Do they enjoy variety and novelty?

If you will be countering strong group norms, be sure that you explain your reasons and the group understands and accepts them. And, finally, be sure that the "creative use of time" is not just for the trainer's benefit.

ACTIVITY

Do a quick review of the time frames for training activities
in your organization in the past year.

How were these time frames decided?

_____

_____

_____

_____

_____

Was it the best choice for the target groups?

_____

_____

_____

_____

What are some options that would work better?

_____

_____

_____

_____

What obstacles will you have to confront to make this
kind of change?

_____

_____

_____

_____

Environment

People are more receptive to learning if they are not too far from their comfort zone. Comfort can come from many sources, both physical and psychological:

- ❏ **The people encountered**—do they know fellow participants? Do they have similar experiences? Are the staff welcoming, open, helpful?
- ❏ **The training site**—ease of access, furniture, lighting, room size, noise, grounds, amenities, unnecessary restrictions.
- ❏ **Domestic concerns**—if it is a residential program, are there arrangements for keeping people in touch with their home environment? Should there be? Is the accommodation basic, deluxe, sumptuous? What recreation is available to occupy people during breaks or evenings? Are special dietary needs considered? Has a smoking policy been set?
- ❏ **Location**—on site or off? Plush or basic? Even if you have your own training facility, there are choices of rooms, use of the grounds, forays into the local area, etc.
- ❏ **Welcoming procedures**—is arriving at the activity made easy or frustrating? Are there refreshments when people get there? Are participants assisted in getting to know each other quickly? Are special personal needs considered?

If you're not sure of the importance of environment, consider the following Case in Point.

Case in Point

The national human resource director of a global banking group arranged a training day for selection interviewing. The general manager for the country was to be among the participants. The consultant who was delivering the course visited the training site the previous week and, together with the human resource director, worked out how the room was to be arranged. The training could be held in the executive dining room, which contained a large mahogany table that took up most of the floor space. For this training, however, they would move the table, leaving only a circle of chairs. This would allow them to set up for various group and skill practice configurations throughout the day. After they decided on the room layout, they ordered the video player, selected the lunch menu, and all seemed well.

On the morning of the training course, the consultant arrived an hour early to find that the room still contained the table and neither the video player nor the human resource director was present. The early morning security staff knew nothing of the plan. By the time everything was put in place, the trainees, general manager among them, were in the room. They stood and watched as furniture was moved, handouts hastily distributed, and equipment installed.

What did this environmental message convey? All that can be confirmed is that on the end-of-day reaction sheet, the general manager commented that the training seemed casual.

Once you've planned the environmental factors, be sure to follow through to ensure they happen, and then let your customers know what they can expect. If you've got these factors right for the intended population, then you have an important selling point to use in publicizing the event. In your descriptive material and in your discussions with prospective participants, let them know what to expect; demonstrate that you have considered their particular needs.

Keep in mind that taking the participant away from the comfort zone *on purpose* can be effective. It has frequently been documented that motivation decreases when people are too comfortable [2], and planning the environment to enhance learning remains completely appropriate. This is not a substitute, however, for lack of attention to detail.

Style

The style of your training initiatives will be formed by the way in which you communicate them, the types of activity you use, and the way(s) in which your trainers deliver them.

Typically, for example, you are likely to send out some preliminary materials or pre-course instructions. Look at the two examples in Figure 5.2. These represent two very different styles for an Introduction to Management course.

Perhaps tradition in your industry or organization or your own professional training has dictated a particular style. However, styles must fit with what you and your organization are trying to do. There

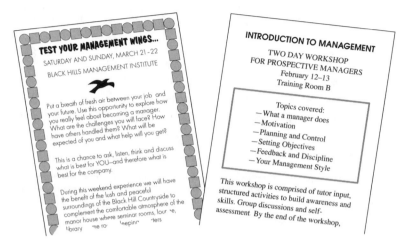

Figure 5.2. Two styles of preliminary material.

are times when a straightforward, no-nonsense approach will be best, and other times when a friendly, informal atmosphere may be better.

Use a verbal style in your printed materials which conveys a clear message about the style that participants will encounter at the training event.

Personal Styles

Which trainer will you use for a particular project? No two trainers are alike, and context considerations demand that you consider how you choose who will work on which kind of project. Personal styles fall into two overall categories: individual and professional. Individually, people behave in ways that are more or less

- ❑ Formal
- ❑ Personal
- ❑ Emotive
- ❑ Assertive
- ❑ Talkative

They have more or less skill in

- ❑ Making the complex simple
- ❑ Drawing people out

❑ "Thinking on their feet"

❑ Adding impromptu examples

❑ Demonstrating visual concept models

The lists are not meant to be exhaustive, simply instructive. Attention to style requires choosing an individual trainer style to suit the customer group [3]. There are different styles of presenting information or instructing that should be considered in terms of what is most appropriate to the situation. Some customer groups may prefer to be taught, while others appreciate a problem-solving approach. Although all good trainers have a bit of a performer in them, some are a laugh a minute and others present in a serious, even earnest manner. We all fall into the trap at one time or another of selecting people who are most like ourselves. You must watch this carefully because it is often necessary to bring in a style different than our own. If your in-house trainers are all of the same mold, perhaps you should work on increasing their awareness and expanding their repertoire. Or you may need to bring in an external training person who meets the need(s) that you desire.

The style of a trainer is a complex interplay between their personality, the training material, the training group, and the organization's culture. As people have different learning styles [4], so do trainers have a range of training styles. For example, some prefer working in a structured way, using short lectures and discussions. Others are able to work more comfortably on skills development, using role play and experiential exercises. Some work best with a very unstructured agenda. It is worth working with your trainers to clarify their training styles, to find out how they work with various activities and customer groups.

Appendix C discusses two trainer style models: the TSI (Training Style Inventory), developed in the 1970s by Richard Brostrom, and a more recent model called FADE developed by David Cleeton. Both analyze style using a four-part model. Depending on which inventory is used, the four styles are: Behaviorist; Humanist; Functionalist and Structuralist or Facilitator; Activator or Demonstrator and Educator. Using this kind of model, you can find out how your trainers prefer various training settings. These models can become a platform for developing a wider set of trainers' skills and enabling your team to project a broad range of professional competence.

This is not the place to discuss the merits of different styles, but to point out that trainer style should be an important consideration when matching context with culture. For example, consider which trainer in your area can work best with senior managers. What is their style? How might other trainers be developed to meet context needs more precisely? What criteria do you apply when recruiting a training officer who might impact context?

ACTIVITY

Take one of your customer groups (Chapter 3) and plot their context needs on a matrix. Think about format, timing, environment, style, and any other headings that are appropriate for the group. For each entry, consider whether you now provide it (or better yet, ask *them*!). If you do not provide for these context needs, brainstorm how you can provide for them in the future.

HOW TO DETERMINE CONTEXT NEEDS

One way is to use your general knowledge and intuition. You will find that you actually know quite a bit about different customer groups beyond what kind of training they want for themselves or their staff. However, the following tips will help you understand the various groups' priorities in training.

Senior Managers Typically Want To

❏ Focus on business results (reduce costs, increase productivity, waste less, expand markets)

❏ Use time effectively

❏ Concentrate on priorities

Mid-Level Managers Typically Want To

❏ Feel useful and important

❏ Be supported when trying new skills

❏ Be appreciated

Individual Contributors or Specialists Typically Want To

❑ Receive acknowledgment of their unique skills

❑ Be treated as special

❑ Be welcomed as a group member

❑ Be introduced to other opportunities within the organization

Lower-Level Staff Typically Want To

❑ Understand where they fit in the "big picture"

❑ See others in the same situation as themselves

❑ See value in any new expectations put on them

You probably also have a pretty good idea about a group's preference for high or low levels of interaction, formality or informality, distaste or appreciation for posh settings. There will be other things—excitement over new ideas, need for a sense of smooth sailing, to always/never be consulted, and so on. These you know from your general interaction with and observation of various individuals and groups in your organization, but through ongoing partnering with your customers, you will gain a more precise understanding. There are many situations that already exist or that you can create to learn more about context needs. Activities for keeping in touch with your customers (Chapter 7) can also be opportunities for extending your antennae. The key is to look, listen, and ask (when appropriate) before, during, and after training experiences. You will soon find your "database" is quite extensive.

HOW TO MARKET CONTEXT

Whether you are discussing a forthcoming training program or sending out written course material, you can advertise some of the context components. Simply stating the course location will sometimes be enough for the prospective attendees to know about it. (They might all be familiar with the twelfth floor conference room; they might also know what to expect if you name a local college or university where you will be holding an event.) If further explanation is needed, give it! Avoid giving people unnecessary concerns.

If the training course you have developed is surprisingly slow to fill up with participants, despite it having been "customer-led" from the start, try to find out what the difficulty is. Perhaps it is a context issue.

Program cost, for example, could also be an issue. *You* may know you are providing great value, but does the customer regard it as a value? You often need to spell it out! And is it worth the money and the time invested—to them? As more training is being charged to line operations instead of being centrally funded, departments are becoming more and more careful of where the money goes. If you learn about a lower-priced training option your customers have identified, perhaps externally, it may be up to you to demonstrate that what you are recommending is a better value *for them*.

If, on the other hand, the value is obvious but the cost is *seen* as too high, is there anything you can do to reduce it? Flexibility is not only a key requirement of modern management, it is essential in providing training.

THE INVESTIGATIVE TRAIL

Despite the fact that this book is not a guide to needs assessment, there is one point worth mentioning that has to do with the investigatory research itself. Since assessing customer need for performance improvement programs should be part of your regular market research, consider whether your *method* fits the cultures you analyze.

In "Detecting Your Research Strategy" [5], Richard Thorpe and Jean Moscarola devised a variation on Kolb's learning styles demonstrating styles of investigation. Their premise is that the various approaches to research are embodied in some famous fictional detectives as shown in Figure 5-3.

We can see from Figure 5-3 that the *outcome* in all cases remains performance-improvement solutions (whether training-based or not), but the *processes* of investigating needs are quite distinct.

Hercule Poirot: Theoretical and Rational

❑ Collect all sorts of relevant information from a range of sources; have a thorough understanding of appropriate models and theories

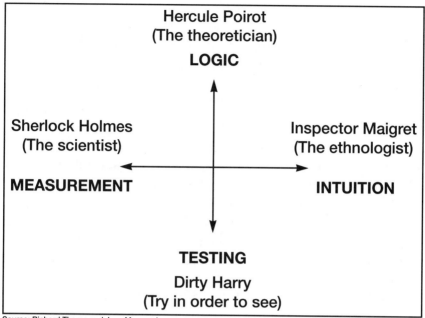

Source: Richard Thorpe and Jean Moscarola

Figure 5-3. Different approaches to analyzing needs.

❑ Apply your own knowledge and expertise

❑ Analyze what you find and infer answers (solutions)

Sherlock Holmes: Scientific

❑ Engage in minute and systematic observation, using either questionnaires (including performance appraisals) or structured interviews

❑ Subject your findings to elaborate statistical analysis

❑ Propose and test hypotheses based on your data

Inspector Maigret: Empirical Intuitive

❑ Spend considerable time in the field

❑ Listen with a view to understanding other perspectives

❑ Avoid prior judgment

❑ Use your network to seek out experts in relevant areas; gain from their experience

Dirty Harry: Action Research

❑ Try something; provoke a reaction

❑ Observe reactions and determine next step

❑ Try something else

More than likely, one of these strategies will suit a particular customer group more than another. Would your senior management respond more to a Holmes approach than a Maigret? Isn't the Dirty Harry approach what many marketing departments do much of the time? It would be dangerous to typecast, however. Start investigating now!

Thorpe and Moscarola point out that good researchers need not only understand which strategy is most appropriate, but should also have some competence in them all.

With this flexibility, your customers will see you as "appropriate" from the start, and that is an important step in building the relationship with your market—enhancing your customer focus.

SUMMARY

In this chapter we explored the context issues—those areas that are added to the specific performance improvement objectives and content of any training and development program to make up the total training experience for your customer. Like non-verbal communication, context issues deliver strong messages, often causing puzzling reactions if we are not aware of the source.

REFERENCES/NOTES

1. Excerpt from "Fast Learning," *Fast Company,* October/November 1996.

2. Bardwick, Judith M., *Danger in the Comfort Zone,* Amacom, 1995.

3. This may mean a complementary style or one that challenges according to your objectives.

4. See Further Reading: David Kolb's or Alan Mumford's and Peter Honey's work on learning style.

5. Thorpe, Richard, and Moscarola, Jean, "Detecting Your Research Strategy," *Management Education and Development,* Vol. 22, Part 2, Association of Management Education and Development, London, 1991.

CHAPTER 6

Your Image— Divining, Defining, and Refining

How the rest of your organization views the training and development function has a significant impact on its effectiveness. Furthermore, determining just what the right image is for your organizational culture will give you a head start in making the right link with your customers.

WHAT IS IMAGE?

In the preceding chapters, we have mentioned image often, without any exploration of what it includes. The role of image in your marketing strategy is a powerful yet often invisible key to the success of your plans. The foundation—the connection with the customer that underlies the image must be there, of course—and the previous chapters should have helped in that area. However, failure to attend to and understand image can lead to puzzling lapses in customer attention and disturbances in otherwise sound customer relationships. Let's start with a simple example that illustrates the importance of image.

Cosmetics and toiletries are sold in a wide variety of outlets, including

❑ Discount drugstore chains
❑ Airports
❑ Beauty salons
❑ Specialist cosmetic boutiques
❑ Mail order catalogs
❑ Major department stores

Think about how major department stores market cosmetics. The customer receives attentive service, an opportunity to try the products, answers to questions—in general, personal attention. Contrast that with how a chain drug store markets the same products. Perhaps you saw an ad in a local circular advising of the drugstore's sale, or you just know you can run in and grab what you need. Drugstores display the items on racks. They expect you to buy with your eyes, to "pick up and pay." There is generally no product information available, and indeed, the drugstore does not expect you to want any.

Imagine what might happen if the drugstore applied the marketing strategies of the department store. You would undoubtedly feel annoyed that the drugstore employees were taking up your valuable time and interfering with your busy Saturday or lunch hour. Some might see it as plain intrusive.

The marketing strategy must respond to the business goals, culture, and the customers of the organization. Whether the image to be conveyed is "pile 'em high and sell 'em cheap" or "we are here to serve you," the message must be clear in order to continue attracting the customers that keep the business alive.

The image people have of the performance improvement team, both personally and professionally, determines how much they respect and accept the messages and solutions that the team creates. Image is in the "eye of the beholder," but there are many things you can do to influence what your customers "behold." Our image of a thing or a person comes from

❏ What we see
❏ What we hear
❏ What we expect

We will now examine these three major components that make up "image."

Outward Appearance

Consider the swan. The generally held image of a swan is of a graceful, well-balanced animal gliding effortlessly along the water. It

is well-known, however, that in actuality, swans exert a lot of effort—
"paddling like hell"—to keep afloat or to get where it's going. Yet,
knowing that doesn't change our image of the swan. It is still found
frequently on brand labels and in logos because it brings to mind a
positive image—of calm competence.

The outward appearance of your training function is made up of
those factors your customers come face to face with, such as

- ❑ How your materials look (their design, style, neatness, conve-
  nience in using)
- ❑ Any memos or other correspondence you send, whether physically or electronically
- ❑ The language, grammar, "user-friendliness" found in communi-
  cation items
- ❑ The range of services you are seen to offer (and the range of
  activities with which you become involved)
- ❑ What any training facility you use looks like (style, neatness,
  cleanliness)
- ❑ How you and your team present yourselves (dress, grooming,
  etc.)
- ❑ How you and your team speak to others (tone, grammar, choice
  of words, relevance)
- ❑ How you and your team listen to others' ideas and suggestions
- ❑ How quickly you respond to requests or criticisms
- ❑ Your *apparent* mood (How do you and your team present yourselves, handle interruptions, respond to uninformed or repetitive
  questions? How do you treat those who fail to follow instructions in a training setting?)
- ❑ And, very importantly, who you recruit and how you are seen to
  train and develop your own team

These are all areas you can influence. Once you determine what
image you want to portray, you will be able to develop ideas for
bringing your outward appearance in line. The following case is
probably just due to the thoughtlessness of the training manager, but
consider the impression it left.

Case in Point

The training manager of a well-known healthcare organization had arranged a meeting of senior staff members. A prominent external consultant had been hired to work with them on some strategic issues. The meeting was set for 5:30 p.m. and was expected to continue until around 8. The consultant arrived shortly before the meeting was to begin and found the room was a mess, with furniture and litter scattered about from the day's activities. There was no one to help the consultant set up or any sign of coffee or snacks. As the participants entered they had no choice but to help arrange the room so they could proceed with the meeting. The organization promotes an image of being both caring and professional; how do you think those involved would view the training department?

Your Reputation

There is a television commercial for the German-built Cadillac Catera which, like many other commercials, demonstrates faith in the power of reputation. Cadillac had been suffering from a tarnished reputation that was costing sales. In trying to change the reputation of a car that was perceived as an "old fogies" vehicle to one that appeals to a new market, the company launched a new commercial with the tag line being: "the Caddy that zigs." What are some of the messages that this line conveys?

—"It's young and sporty." (If I drive one, I'll be/look/feel young and sporty.)

—"It will be good for *me—make me feel alive.*" (If I drive one, I'll "zig" also.)

—"They're up-to-date." (It's not my grandfather's car anymore.)

— "They value fun." (Driving it will be pleasurable, easy—not hard work.)

Over time, these responses to the campaign—none of which deals with concrete, factual information—are meant to change the reputation of the car in the minds of its intended market.

Another example of the subtle ways reputation is affected can be seen in the "Ruby" campaign of the cosmetics firm The Body Shop.

"Ruby" is the name that has been coined for the rather Rubenesque doll, which was designed to convey the message that women should enjoy and accept how they actually look instead of how fashion magazines and designers dictate. However, advertising campaigns are not cheap and marketing budgets are not spent altruistically. If this message succeeds, what underpins it is the intended message that:

—"The Body Shop understands and values ME." (Therefore, I shall buy their products).

Where does your reputation come from?

- ❑ **Memory**—from previous contact with your function
- ❑ **"Gossip"**—what people say about your function
- ❑ **"Stamp of approval"**—*who else* values and respects what your function has done

What others say about you obviously depends to a great degree on their perception of their experiences with you. You cannot control their perceptions. You can to some degree control their experiences, however. You can monitor what you think are your customers' perceptions; ask for feedback, respond positively and, whenever possible, work hard to create those impressions you want them to take away.

FOR YOU TO THINK ABOUT:

Who has your ear?

Do others see you to represent any particular group?

Do they see you to be in a position of influence within the organization?

Do they see you as included at corporate strategy level?

Recently, the chief executive of a large retail food group in the UK said that the role of human resources was key to staying successful in the current business climate. The HR function was often to "help him [the chief executive] justify his attention to people, actively support change (not sit on the fence waiting to be told what to do), and to provide an absolutely trustworthy and confidential ear." He acknowledged, however, that many of his peers had not yet realized the vital role human resources plays.

Even if you have not made it into the senior management circle, consider the level of influence at which others see you. If you instituted a major change when you began your job, or you created the current training and development function yourself, you may have to work hard and patiently to let people know how it is different from what existed before. If you have re-focused your previous role to a set of new goals and ways of operating (for example, moving from being a course provider to an internal consultant), your task will be harder. You don't have the advantage of nationwide television commercials to send out your message, so you will have to educate at every turn to counteract the images attached to the previous role.

The Mental Picture

A mental picture is even more subjective than reputation. It is based on assumptions, misconceptions, the other person's frame of mind, their memory, and their prejudices. The phrase "You're only as good as your last act" comes to mind here. Mental pictures are made of impressions imprinted on our minds. Sometimes one impression can wipe out another, or, for whatever reason, one impression can cast a deep and lingering mark. This can work both to your advantage and disadvantage. Moments when mental pictures get "taken" include times of

❑ Emotional crisis

❑ Embarrassment

❑ Physical downturns

❑ Great importance

❑ Great anticipation

❑ Recollection (when something you do or say reminds the other of someone else or another situation)

Politicians, the media, and the advertising world constantly try to alter the mental pictures we have. Think about some scandal, which a few years later, is forgotten. Does anyone in the U.S. still avoid Tylenol because it was subjected to horrific poisonings several years ago? Careful media relations accompanied remedial acts to obliterate the event. On the other hand, without careful handling, negative images can persist indefinitely. There are still people who avoid buying Exxon gasoline to fill up their cars because of the way the company handled the 1989 oil spill off Alaska, which left many people with a negative impression of the company's concern for the environment.

In its simplest form, an apology is an example of an attempt to alter one person's mental picture of another. While you cannot control the creation of the mental pictures that make up the image people have of you, you can try and learn what they are and counter them with new actions.

Lastly, consider the time it takes to develop a positive mental image—one of trust and integrity, for instance. And how long it takes to change it to a negative one? Conversely, it takes extremely little time to set a negative image in place and quite a long time to convert it to a positive one.

What Does Your Organization Think of the Training and Development Function?

People can sometimes be amazingly blind to the truth. It is easy to think that because we are "something," people will recognize it. The truth is that often this is not the case. People who are dedicated may be seen as zealous or do-gooders. Those who work hard to be professional may be seen as aloof or too interested in theory. Finding out what your customers really think will be extremely helpful in your efforts to position your function in the most effective way.

There are several ways you can gather clues to the image(s) others have of you. You can make assumptions based on who returns your calls and how quickly. You can reflect on what meetings, task groups, policy issues you are invited to contribute to. You can review the enrollment numbers of your training activities and try to learn the reasons for any abnormalities. Your budget often indicates how those who control the company's purse strings perceive the training function.

Activity

On the left side of a piece of paper list adjectives to describe the image you hope you are promoting. Fold the paper so you can't see what you've written. On the right hand side, list adjectives describing how you think your organization perceives you.

Compare the two lists. Then discuss your conclusions with your team and with some of your customers. Obviously, this activity will only be useful if you are completely honest with yourself.

Of course another way to find out what your customers think of you is to ask them directly, and if you have built a relationship based on open communication, they should be willing to tell you. To make that process a bit easier, however, we have included a Training Image Survey in Appendix B for you to distribute to some or all of your customer groups.

The training image survey

To get the most useful information, you should ensure that some of your sponsors and influencers—champions, blockers, *and* doomsayers—complete it, as well as some direct customers. The survey is based purely on perception and requires very little time to complete. The survey results will ultimately reveal that others perceive the training department as more or less:

❑ **Reactive**—being seen mainly to provide, refer, seek out on request, and driven by the immediate demands of the situation

❑ **People-driven**—highly concerned with individuals' development

❑ **System-driven**—highly concerned with providing the skills needed for the jobs in a systematic, ordered way

❑ **Strategic**—taking a broader, more long-term view; pro-active, planning activities and processes to strengthen the business while not losing sight of the importance of people to make that happen

WHAT IS THE "RIGHT" IMAGE?

While ultimately the training function needs to reflect the business strategy to be of optimum benefit to the organization, all of these modes have a value at some times. It may even be prudent to be perceived as people-driven to one group and system-driven to another. The main point is to know the image you want to portray and know how to promote it.

It's easy to throw around words like "professional" or "business-driven," but often different people attach different meanings to these words. Words are a good place to start in planning your image, as long as defined actions support them. It is useful to create a list of words that support your values as a training function and as individuals within it. This will help you define the image you want to promote.

However, choosing the right components of "image" needs to include what the customer wants. A trap many "suppliers" fall into is thinking they know best. Your image is like a bakery window: even when you are hungry, if the window display shows only cakes, cookies, and pies when what you really crave is bread, or if it intimidates you with its formality, or looks a bit messy or even dirty—in some way doesn't meet your expectations—you will never go inside and taste the truly wonderful items their market research told them you wanted. So just as you have listened and fine-tuned the "product" to match needs, you must attend to your image with the same care.

One of your customer groups may respond best to friendly, informal approaches, where another would be put off by them, relating more readily to someone who seems serious, efficient, and knowledgeable. As you have come to know the various personalities within your organization, you will be able to track what kind of image generates the best response from them.

One way of approaching the task of defining your image is to give yourself an "image workshop." This works best with a team and could ideally include some cooperative customers.

ACTIVITY

Image Workshop

Step 1

Identify five important customer/customer groups (see Chapter 3) and write their names across the top of a page (or flip chart). Draw column lines between them. It might look something like this:

Marketing Department	Customer Service Managers	Production Supervisors	Finance Department	Senior Management Team

Step 2

For each customer group, generate a list of descriptive words—generally adjectives are best—to indicate how you think that customer group would like to perceive you. If you split this step between groups of team members, it is best to have each part of the team focus on at least two customer groups. This ensures specificity. Your lists might look something like this:

Marketing Department	Customer Service Managers	Production Supervisors	Finance Department	Senior Management Team
flexible	knowledgeable	down-to-earth	well-qualified	outward looking
innovative	approachable	talks our language	knowledgeable	knows business
responsive	easy to talk to	interested in us	efficient	persuasive
friendly	responsive	understands us	serious.	up-to-date
sense of humor	jargon-free	informal	accessible	quick thinking
understands us	good presence	adds value	quick response	cost-conscious
etc.	etc.	etc.	etc.	etc.

Step 3

Now the whole team should focus on one customer or customer group list at a time. First, take a good look at the list; make sure you're all clear about meanings; link up similar items and group others. Cross out any you change your mind about. Make any necessary changes to improve clarity. Choose the five most important descriptors, and for each one, *brainstorm ways in which you can demonstrate this quality* in your external image—your "outward appearance." For example:

WELL-QUALIFIED -
hang any certificates in training area
write short biographies—newsletter, training
materials
KNOWLEDGEABLE -
get article published
stress what you know in publicity materials
SERIOUS
use "formal" typefaces
avoid glossy phrases or "cute" comments
send written messages, answers, announcements
follow up
make appointments; have agendas
etc.

INFORMAL
have frequent brief contact:
call and ask what's been happening
drop by department periodically
wander around and see what's
happening
use friendly language in materials
invite them to your turf
UNDERSTANDS US -
use realistic scenario in publicity
spend part of a day in department
invite collaboration
etc.

It might be even more powerful if these words were derived from customers by using an interview technique like a repertory grid. [1]

Step 4

Now you are ready to make a plan. What things will be easy to do? Which will take more resources? To what standard will you do them? Use your planning skills to develop an action plan and set a date to review progress and results in three months (or an appropriate length of time for your purposes).

Alternatively, you may determine (in much the same fashion) *how you'd like others to see you,* and then carefully assess each customer group against your results. Are the right items presented in the right way in *your* cosmetic department or bakery window? Will they want to come in and buy?

You may find that you have to work on yourselves personally as well as your publicity. One training department, in response to an exercise similar to this image workshop, put itself through an intensive presentation skills workshop. Even though the team was made up of skilled trainers, they realized they needed work on persuasive presentations. They went on to consult an image advisor (the personal rather than the corporate variety) who gave them tips on personal presentation to help them look the part as well. This may seem less than important faced with the pressures of running training day to day, but when the stakes are acceptance vs. being marginalized, it becomes an effort worth taking. While this attention to the "look of things" may go against the grain for some people, it may help to remember that visual appearance accounts for around 55 percent of the initial impression we make. It *does* make a difference.

HOW CAN YOU BE ALL THINGS TO ALL PEOPLE?

You can't. However, depending on your team size and resources, you can—and must—do *some* degree of targeted marketing activities. If you are writing about a particular training event, use words and style that will be acceptable to the target population. There is no reason it has to be in the same format as every other piece of publicity. You may determine that you need to fit into broad categories of image, for example, one for senior management, one for line management, and one for operations-level staff. This may mean you have to compile three sets of course directories or have three templates in your desktop publishing system for training materials. Often departments do not even think of varying their format for their audience. Unfortunately, too often training sees itself bound by corporate policy; when in fact, there is usually plenty of room for creativity in promoting your image.

Case in Point

In one major service company, senior managers were reluctant to attend a relevant and necessary presentation skills workshop offered to the entire management population. Middle managers reported enthusiastically on the workshop in every way. By changing the image; renaming the course "advanced presentation skills workshop"; citing new benefits, which included a "personal consultation" to discuss individual needs; and individually mailing details to the senior managers, attendance improved 400 percent. The training department, however, did not really change the content from the earlier workshop.

Allow Your Image to Evolve

Whatever image you choose, it is important to allow it to evolve over time and to remain open to the possibility of alteration if needed. Images can and do change: remember the swan began life as an "ugly duckling." There is a danger, however, of getting too mechanistic when tinkering with image and losing sight of its purpose—to attract your customers. *They* are dynamic; so must your image be.

SUMMARY

This chapter discussed the basis of "image"—those things you can control easily and some that you cannot. There is an "Image Workshop" through which you and your team and ideally, your customers, can analyze and then choose the image(s) you want to create and then plan what to do to promote that image.

NOTES

1. Repertory Grid is an interviewing technique used to categorize experiences and people according to an individual's "personal constructs." The technique, developed by an American clinical psychologist, George Kelly, was first introduced in *The Psychology of Personal Constructs* in 1955.

    Two people have written widely of its use in management and HRD. One is Dr. Valerie Stewart who introduced Repertory Grid as part of the process of defining what we would now call management competencies. Her book *Business Applications of Repertory Grid* was first published in 1983 and is now available on the internet at http://www.enquirewithin.co.nz/ business.htm. The other is Dr. Mark Easterby-Smith, who wrote about using it to measure training needs and evaluate management training. He wrote *How to Use Repertory Grids in HRD* in 1980, which was published as a special issued of the *Journal of European Industrial Training* in 1980. "Using repertory grids in management," a revised version, appears in the *Journal of European Industrial Training*, Vol. 20, No. 3, 1996, pp. 3–30.

CHAPTER 7

Maintaining Your Marketing Focus— the Long Term

To benefit in the long term from all the hard work you have done, you need to maintain your marketing focus. At its simplest, this means always keeping the customer in mind. Specifically, it means constantly defining and highlighting what the customer benefits will be.

We have covered the basics fairly well, and you may already have some ideas for improving the marketing of training and development in your organization. In Chapter 3, you explored ways to identify your customer groups, and define your priority targets. Chapter 4 examined the value and methodology of building customer relationships. Chapter 5 looked at the importance of understanding the content and context needs of your customers. Chapter 6 revealed some important things about the influence image can have on training effectiveness, and offered some suggestions of ways to review where you are, and how you want others to perceive you.

The next step in the process is one that must become a constant effort, closely linked to the daily activity of everyone in the performance improvement function. Despite pressures from deadlines or senior management, other peoples' needs, pet projects, hard-to-refuse requests, and other day-to-day realities, you should maintain your focus on marketing your function in everything you do. Maintaining your marketing focus, so that it stays customer-oriented, breaks down into five areas:

☐ Ensure that you have identified the needs of your target customers

☐ Promote your service via benefits that match your customers' needs

☐ Make the most of your network of communication links

☐ Stay visible and add value in everything you try to do

☐ Build and improve relationships constantly with your customers

Ensure that You Have Identified Customer Needs

Once you are satisfied that you have correctly identified your customers' content and context needs, it is all too easy to assume that what has worked successfully in the past will still be acceptable in the future. This is a dangerous assumption. As the pace of change has increased in modern organizations, tolerance for outmoded ideas or methods is practically nil.

Only by being in touch with the business realities, day to day, can a training and development function hope to recognize how to adapt. Recognizing the changing needs of your customer groups (and, of course, acting on that recognition) is the only way to avoid being marginalized. Your internal processes must be formulated to recognize that accurate intelligence is the key to marketing success.

Promote via Benefits

Promotion is about raising awareness and encouraging uptake through publicity and personal communication. Successful promotion is based on benefits derived from an understanding of your customers' needs, and how they can be met. Any salesperson worthy of that name will tell you that benefits answer the question "So what?" (or "how will that change things for me?" or "what will it really mean to me?").

Every sales trainer learns to distinguish between features and benefits, and passes this vital information to sales trainees. The trainees go on the road firmly believing that benefits sell and features often do not. Despite this effort, many salespeople still pump out a list of features, in the mistaken belief that they are doing a good job. It's the same in training. To take one simple example, a feature statement about one of your training events might be:

New course times: 2–5 p.m. Tuesday and Thursday . . .

For certain customers, with specific needs, we can turn this into a valuable benefit, which might look something like:

Course times are altered to Tuesday and Thursday afternoons, 2–5 p.m, so that you can still meet your morning deadlines and stay on top of incoming orders.

Benefits are what people buy, not features. Most sales trainers can probably quote Charles Revson, the founder of Revlon Cosmetics, who said in the 1930s: "we don't sell lipsticks; we sell dreams."

It's so easy to take the benefits for granted, and forget to include them in your promotional material once you have incorporated them into your training design or plan. Sometimes we make a common mistake of assuming the benefits will be obvious, but this is definitely an occasion when stating the obvious is essential. Part of your marketing plan must be to relate specific benefits to your customer groups, and remind them of what they are getting.

ACTIVITY

What follows is a list of frequent training "features" often included in program descriptions, or in training conversations. Try your hand at changing at least half of them into benefit statements. As you do so, for each one, try to have a particular customer group in mind.

FEATURES	BENEFITS
• Over a working lunch . . .	
• Complete teams are included . . .	

• Short modules . . .	
• Highly participative . . .	
• Periodic review days . . .	
• Telephone help available . . .	
• Competency-based . . .	
• Virtual classroom . . .	
• Course begins on Sunday evening . . .	
• Group includes managers from each country . . .	
• Our trainers are all line managers . . .	

Hint: If you can still say "so what?" to your benefit statement, try going a step further.

For example, take the feature statement: "self-contained open learning package" and ask yourself: So what?

"So learners can work at their own pace in the workplace." *So what?*

"So busy work periods will not be interrupted." *So what?*

"So you will get improved skills from your staff without having to send them out of the office, which would require costly replacements with temporary staff or overtime."

A good benefit statement might then be:

"Designed to be used in the workplace so your staff can improve their skills during the slack times, saving you the expense of hiring temporary replacements or paying employees for overtime."

Examples of Benefits Statements

FEATURES	BENEFITS
• Over a working lunch . . .	*People won't have to lose work time to learn*
• Complete teams are included . . .	*Offers an immediate shared language and understanding*
• Short modules . . .	*Can be fit into any type of schedule*
• Highly participative . . .	*People will leave having experienced the learning, making it much easier to apply*
• Periodic review days . . .	*Brush-ups couldn't be easier; individual issues can be addressed*
• Telephone help available . . .	*Get answers when YOU need them*
• Competency-based . . .	*Training is directly tied to performance criteria; can be self-assessed*
• Virtual classroom . . .	*No need to spend time/money on travel; people can work at their own sites*
• Course begins on Sunday evening . . .	*Time to get to know other participants; no rush-hour traveling*
• Group includes managers from each country . . .	*Opportunity to learn how other cultures operate; make worldwide career connections*
• Our trainers are all line managers . . .	*Content will be credible and practical; reality-based*

Sales trainees are taught to construct benefit statements by stating a feature and then adding "which means that . . ." For example: "we offer open learning packages, which means that inexperienced staff can work at their own pace, under local supervision." You and your team should make benefits clear both in writing and in face-to-face communication.

MAKE THE MOST OF YOUR COMMUNICATION LINKS

There are many opportunities for trainers to communicate with the rest of the organization on a regular basis. A marketing focus requires you to examine and plan some of these opportunities so that you can make the best use of them. The best place to start is with your existing team. You may want to do some sort of networking exercise, to see how much impact your department has on the organization. See Appendix D for an example of such an activity.

When you have determined who you know, and who you would like to know better, you can start looking at ways to communicate effectively with your targets, and ways to collate the intelligence gathered from the activity. It is a good idea to allocate specific responsibility for different groups to individuals or small teams in your department, and to discuss your reasons for targeting particular people and groups. Your own experience will tell you who is capable of what, and it is also worth remembering that this can be a good development activity for inexperienced trainers.

When you have a clear idea of the "who," you can start looking at some "hows"'—the following are a few ideas.

One-to-One (Face-to-Face and Telephone)

❑ CWA (Communicate by Walking Around). One approach is to make a concerted effort to visit every manager over a period of, say, three months. The visit should be informal, perhaps arranged the same morning ("I'm going to be in your area, do you have time for a cup of coffee?") or chanced without prior arrangement. These informal chats can be invaluable for introducing what you are doing and finding out what they need. The lack of formality helps keep the managers at ease—nothing particular will be expected of them.

This activity is especially useful for promoting fledgling training functions or when the training manager is new and needs to meet as many people as possible.

❑ "Blue folders." One training manager keeps a special "blue folder" for each of the 20 senior managers. It includes a checklist of who spoke to whom when, what was done, and what needs to be done. See Figure 7-1.

❑ Similarly, you can keep a file on each manager and make an effort to either see or speak to them on the phone at least once a quarter. Note down any relevant information that you should follow up on before the next contact.

❑ Visit with those who don't seem friendly. "Trainers find it easy to spend time with a friendly face—they listen and make a good impression. However, it is often much more important to put the time into cultivating [relationships with] the less friendly faces. You need to win some of them over if your influence is to grow," said one training manager.

	John Doe
Jan 14	Discussed role, Reviewed managment training "no needs"
March 3	Asked for info re: mentoring skills
March 4	Sent book list and info re: one-on-one coaching
March 7	Called re: receipt—follow up in 2 weeks
March 22	Enrolled in coaching program; discussed concerns re: team leader vacancies—referred him to Sarah D.
April 19	Sent Wall Street Journal article on mentoring programs

Figure 7-1. Example of "Blue folder" notes.

Meetings

You or your departmental representative should have a clear purpose for attending different departments' meetings. You might be there to gather information about strategic decisions, to cement a relationship, to seek reactions to something you are planning or have already done, to lobby on behalf of a particular activity you wish to pursue, to present ideas formally or informally, to listen to the climate of the meeting, or some other reason, perhaps several.

❑ Attendance at key management meetings. One company includes training on the agenda at every third departmental management meeting, and a representative from the training department sits in. Following the meeting, the training person reports back to the department on any actions taken or planned as a result of the meeting.

❑ "Exclusive" invitational events. One training manager instituted "diners' clubs"—monthly lunches (invitation only) to a selection of senior managers from throughout the company. At each event a trainer presented some topic of interest and also talked about what else the training department had been involved in. Sometimes the topics came from the managers and sometimes the training manager used his/her "sixth sense" to plan one. The results were many:

— the managers felt "looked after" by the training manager;

— there was an opportunity to discuss management development on a company-wide basis in an unrushed and informal manner;

— the training manager was able to stay in tune with current concerns;

— several managers were enticed through this process to participate in the design or delivery of future management training; and

— they became receptive and supportive of training initiatives in general.

❑ Individual needs analysis. The sales training manager of one multinational organization sets up a system in which he or a member of his HRD team, armed with their course listing, visits every company employee once every six months for a one-to-one training needs analysis. Such a meeting takes about 45 minutes and the employee's local manager is present. By the end of the session, there is an agreement between the manager and the employee as to the type of training activities the individual will engage in during the forthcoming six months [1].

❑ Turn your annual training strategy discussions into a mini-conference. Consider an off-site location, and invite influential guest speakers from inside and outside the organization to meet and discuss HR concerns, in a training context. Ask them to speak on a special topic that will add value to your event and generate interest in what you are doing. Include invitations to line managers and others who might be influential in supporting your initiatives for the future, and also consider asking some of your detractors (the blockers and doomsayers) to attend—putting them in influential peer groups can be very useful.

Information Technology

❑ Issue a virtual bulletin regularly to update people. An online newsletter that mentions what is happening in training works well, if the culture is right, and it gives you the opportunity to reinforce customer benefits. You can include contact names, so those wanting more information can obtain it.

❑ If your organization does not have e-mail, send out material on floppy disks, which are inexpensive. This medium may be more appealing than another newsletter disappearing into a heap of paper. You can make the disks interactive by including questionnaires, surveys or contests.

❑ If your organization has an intranet, use it to display upcoming training events, explaining how the training will help people to be more effective; incorporate testimonials, surveys, registration forms.

❑ Match your information technology (IT) services to the culture of your organization—perhaps become a leader in using the technology, but take care not to frighten off those who are resisting the IT revolution.

❑ You can also use e-mail for daily or weekly "training updates" where you announce current activities, plans, booking information, changes to previously scheduled events, etc. You may have to publicize the e-mail updates by another medium until customers get used to automatically looking at it.

Paper-Based Methods

Caution! It has been proven time and time again: people don't read! They glance; they guess; they assume; they plan to read it. If you choose to market with a print medium, it will have a better chance of being read if you

> ⇒ *Use short, vivid words*
> ⇒ *Repeat important details often*
> ⇒ *Illustrate with catchy pictures or charts*
> ⇒ *Use gimmicks (e.g., contests) to encourage more thorough investigation*
> ⇒ *Follow up with telephone calls when appropriate*

Here are some paper-based ideas that have worked:

❑ A manufacturing plant's employees enjoy the quarterly newsletter, *Training News*, published by the training department. It includes photographs of employees in various training activities, whether classroom-based or not, as well as articles about new or unusual development offerings. Individuals who have benefitted from training and development activities, including executive-level participants, write articles from their own point of view. This newsletter also includes the intricacies of recruiting the right kind of person to carry out the training role. It also lists future training plans and discusses training and development strategy. Sometimes it carries short pieces highlighting people in the training and development team—their background, special interests, and some personal details—so that other employees perceive them as fully dimensional colleagues.

❑ In another company, six weeks before a training program, the training manager sends out a single sheet "advertising" it. This advertisement describes why the program has been developed and who the prospective participants are. He then encourages them to ask for details and register by e-mail. It is a very successful way to remind people of what has been planned in just enough time for them to arrange to attend.

❑ Another company periodically circulates a matrix showing graphically an overview of the company management development plan. It includes what is offered for each level, objectives, who should and should not participate, relevant dates, as well as other activities such as mentoring opportunities, self-study modules, etc.—all on one double-sized piece of paper. An attachment lists skills or knowledge areas (previously identified as crucial for development) and matches them to the particular course or activity. Again, it invites prospective participants to contact the training department for further details or to register for any of the activities.

❑ Similarly, at another company, the training department graphically represents a "development path"—the "steps" (modules or series of modules) that individuals must take in sequence to achieve different levels within the company. The diagram appears in the front of the course catalog and is also included in trainee packs at training events.

❑ Through developing a good working relationship with the communications officer, the training manager in one organization has a regular "Training and Development Column" in the company newsletter.

Other paper-based ways to market the training and development function are

❑ Use attractive flyers—identifiable by your department logo and/or type of paper—and place them in strategic spots throughout the company: in the front lobby, outside the restaurant, by the water cooler, in the photocopy room, and so on. Just remember to have a system for updating them so that they always advertise future events. One company has special wall receptacles for these, and employees know to look there to find out what's coming up in training that might be of use to them.

❏ If you produce a training directory, include a tear-off sheet with plenty of white space so recipients can suggest what kind of learning activities interest them.

❏ Course-material packs provide opportunities for various kinds of communication. A list of future events; a set of training personnel profiles, and an invitation for collaboration on various training projects are just some of what you can insert into participant packs.

❏ Similarly, if you routinely have trainees complete training evaluation forms of some sort, you can build on those with specific follow-up information.

STAYING VISIBLE AND ADDING VALUE

It is one thing to solve performance problems through training. It's quite another to have others in the organization perceive that your training programs are beneficial. If those who do not participate in training can see the benefits that training has given to others and the added value that it has produced in the organization, you will go a long way in establishing a successful training and development function. This means that besides meeting the most important employee-training needs or addressing the highest payoff areas, you should on a regular basis do what might be called "internal community work." Some examples follow:

❏ Implement a help-line to support new initiatives, or new materials. One retail company offers an extensive range of distance learning packages. It backs this up with a confidential help-line service, to answer questions, which is available at certain times of the day. The equivalent of after-sales service.

❏ Offer a coaching service or conduct workshops on consulting skills to other providers of internal services (e.g., the information systems department). Do this on a low-cost basis (e.g., lunchtime sessions, presentations plus reading material, a "hotline," etc.).

❏ Facilitate team meetings and demonstrate your skill(s) at getting people to make decisions and achieve results.

❏ Offer confidential counseling (one-to-one) to senior managers, who might resist attending group events, to discuss areas of vulnerability. This can foster a valuable relationship and an opportunity to influence strategic direction and gain useful intelligence.

❏ Distribute desktop "cheat sheets" on subjects like communicating on the telephone, writing pithy memos, managing time, developing employees, and so on. Use small, plasticized cards, which are cheap to set up. This service keeps your department's name in front of people.

❏ Offer other areas where you have developed expertise; for example, develop customer satisfaction surveys for other departments.

❏ Create a career-management resource library. Materials will not be hard to find as there is a wealth of self-study materials available (CBT programs, workbooks, etc.). Let people know it is available.

❏ Seek out speaking and writing opportunities where you will be able to talk about the things you have accomplished.

❏ Seek active involvement for you and your team on corporate task forces or project teams—even if they do not directly impact the training function.

❏ Hold periodic "open houses" and invite the entire organization so they can

— Talk to the training and development team

— View training materials

— Sample course activities

— Explore training video and book resources

— Talk to others who have benefitted from particular development initiatives

— Have one-to-one discussions or make appointments to discuss their particular needs

❏ You can also hold a "smaller" version of the open house such as monthly hour-long "training mornings."

❏ Use information technology (e-mail, intranet) to issue "Topic Briefings" that cover subjects of known interest. Of course, you can also issue these briefings on paper. Aim to provide things people will be surprised, but pleased, to see.

❑ Assemble representative groups of stakeholders to

— Periodically review training output and effectiveness

— Determine success levels to be measured in proposed training and development programs

— Give feedback on training facilities, resources, publicity, etc.

❑ Identify areas where what you are doing is superior to what your counterparts in competitor organizations are doing, and publicize this in your organization.

❑ Get involved in or sponsor research, either in your organization or across company lines. There are always projects looking for sponsors from local academic institutions, training or other professional organizations, or other bodies.

❑ Set up special interest, or cross-functional groups to discuss key HR issues of the day—perhaps as a kind of club or society. Many organizations have used this kind of mechanism, formally or informally, to promote what training can achieve.

There is probably no end to ideas on how your training and development function can stay visible while adding value. There are just three key rules to keep in mind:

> *1. Always do at least a bit more than is expected.*
> *2. Never commit to what you cannot deliver.*
> *3. Seek to add value in every activity.*

SUMMARY

This chapter looked at ways to develop and maintain a customer-oriented focus through a range of activities. It provided ideas for staying visible in a positive way and for improving the way in which you meet your customers' needs. You can build on these suggestions to meet the special needs of your own organization and its culture.

In addition, this chapter also suggested how you can spot and promote the benefits that are right for your priority customers and how to get feedback and use it as a basis for action.

NOTES

1. It is fair to say that this type of individual training needs assessment might surface preferences rather than need. However, a skilled training manager with well-honed interviewing techniques could probe for business-related needs and look for "evidence" to justify need for training. Do not, however, take this as the preferred way to assess training needs.

CHAPTER 8

The Importance of Administration

Training and development—or performance improvement in general—is a service, and like most services it needs to be promoted, "sold," and differentiated from similar services. In the last chapter we talked about ways in which we could promote training effectively. This chapter focuses on the "selling" side, particularly to the way in which you maintain customer focus during delivery of a performance improvement program.

A major supermarket proprietor once quipped "Retail is detail." He meant that his stores should be right in every way—from polished doors as you enter the store, to friendly assistants who help you carry groceries to your car. Everything had to be right so that your shopping experience had no rough edges. A chief executive from a different industry said that your complete experience should be "seamless."

Every meeting with a customer is a "moment of truth," said Jan Carlzon, who has restored the fortunes of more than one airline. On the telephone or face to face, the reputation of an organization can be made or destroyed in those short interactions with the customer. Just as a derogatory word, or a piece of inaccurate information can do irreparable damage, a few positive actions can cement a business relationship for life.

Imagine for a moment that you are calling a hotel to book meeting space for a training program. How well do the hotel employees deal with your request? Do they ask all the right questions? Do they know the answers to your queries? Are you passed from person to person?

Do they offer things you need? Do they quote accurate prices without a lot of checking and cross-checking? Do they add a lot of unexpected extras in the price quote?

This is the personal service you receive in the first "moments of truth," and as you probably know, it sets your expectations for what is to come. What happens when you arrive at the hotel? Are they expecting you at the reception desk? Can they find the details? Do they know what arrangements have been made? Are catering arrangements confirmed? Are you escorted around the premises, and introduced to key staff? Do they explain how to use equipment? Are telephones and restrooms pointed out? Do they add any special touches to make you feel particularly welcome?

How often do you find these experiences "seamless?" When was the last time a course site exceeded your expectations? If you have found a site this good, their success is probably the result of first-class communication processes supported by a committed team. Unfortunately, more often you meet a string of minor annoyances. The site works hard to correct them, but at the end of the day, you feel slightly frustrated and wonder if it is worth using them again. This is an all too familiar story.

One consulting firm faxes the commercial training sites with a list of simple requirements when booking, and asks for confirmation that their requirements can be met—things like room sizes, catering arrangements, equipment, etc. Even when the facility confirms that they will meet the requirements, problems continue to arise.

The question to ask now is obvious—is your own training and development function guilty of some of the same things? Perhaps not to the same degree, you might respond—perhaps defensively. Now is the time to take a long hard look at what your administration really looks like from the outside. Let's start from the beginning and examine each aspect of the administration procedure.

CUSTOMER-FRIENDLY SYSTEMS

Are you easy to do business with? Are your systems designed with the customers' needs in mind rather than your own? Specifically,

❏ Is there a system for recording and following up on customers' requests?

❑ Is paperwork sent out at the right time?

❑ Are phone calls ALWAYS returned?

❑ Are complaints welcomed as opportunities to do better?

These systems should also be useful to you when you need to review the uptake of your customer services.

One training manager sends an annual report to each department head showing who participated in what training over the past year, what the total budget was, what requests were not able to be met, what plans are afoot to pick these requests up and what it would cost. All this information is easily retrieved from the training department's "system" whether a commercially available one, or "home-made."

Professional Standards

Part of your image development work should include setting standards for your administrative procedures. For instance, one company has a rule never to use internal envelopes—the kind that requires you to cross out the past recipient's name and write in the current recipient's name. In fact that company always uses typed labels on their envelopes, rather than hand writing them, as they believe this sets the professional tone they want.

The same company that admittedly depends more on paper systems than many companies today, also sends only original memos, rather than photocopies with a circulation list. With the "mail merge" capability a basic component of virtually all current word processing software, this is an easy standard to uphold, and an easy way to make the recipient feel special. You may argue it is more costly—and you're probably right—but is it really more costly than a poor reputation for quality?

Training Directories and Calendars

Many organizations have moved away from the traditional course catalog, but surprisingly many companies still produce them in some form. If you do, you need to ensure the message is not: "This is all we do"—unless, of course, it is, in which case use caution because that is a sign that your training and development function may be struggling.

The following tips will help you make your directories and calendars customer-friendly:

- ❏ Proofread carefully—sloppiness in print is perceived as symptomatic of operations in general.
- ❏ Use large type and spacing, so people can skim the text—few people will take the time to read it fully!
- ❏ Use plenty of white space to draw attention to the printed parts (Remember—people don't read!)
- ❏ If the budget allows, seek professional publishing expertise. High quality is vital.
- ❏ Mention frequently (on each page) that you can tailor training to suit particular needs.
- ❏ Show (graphically) training sequences that can build careers.
- ❏ Use plenty of graphics, but make sure they suit the culture—photos of real people, cartoons, and stylized symbols all carry different messages.

Case in Point

Brian, the head of training and development for a large travel company, used to produce annual course listings that were well-designed and illustrated, bound and glossy, commensurate with the first-class service the company promoted to its customers. He was proud of the product and often received compliments for the professional-looking document. When the last recession hit, however, he found the image portrayed by the glossy brochure was contrary to the experience of the employees who were all undergoing "belt tightening." Many began to see training as a luxury and attendance dropped. He decided to move "down-market" to a neatly designed but basic sheaf of papers, stapled in the corner and sent out in a simple folder. Interest increased dramatically and he attributes this to producing a sense of "oneness" between the training function and the rest of the company—demonstrating that training and development was, in fact, a necessity, not a luxury.

Course Announcements

Whatever form of announcement you use, it is important that it sets the right tone—both the one you want to set and the one that truly represents what the reader will receive. In addition, you should make sure the announcement includes how and where to get more information about the program.

In most organizations, it is common to provide contact names on the publicity material. Make sure extension numbers are correct, and include fax, e-mail, etc. Also make sure that your announcements clearly cover the following essentials:

❑ The title or subtitle of the event should reflect the topic in some way. It's surprising how confusing some titles can be.

❑ Indicate the target group.

❑ Mention who should *not* participate.

❑ Describe what the program objectives are and benefits to the participants.

❑ Delineate the subject areas the course will cover.

❑ Explain the methodology to be used (unless you have a particular reason for not saying at this point).

❑ Alert readers where the event will be held, whether it is residential or not, and possibly

—the program length

—arrival and departure times

—briefing requirements

—the time needed to do any pre-work

Some of these last details may appear instead in pre-program information you send to registrants, but they must be spelled out clearly and reinforced at key points along the communication trail.

Booking Procedures

The golden rule is flexibility. While you obviously want every course full and no late cancellations, try to acknowledge that business problems can interfere with training activities, no matter how much they are needed. Support people by offering alternative dates, and do not insist that applications should be on the proper registration form. You may have a special registration form for training programs. Specially designed registration forms certainly offer advantages:

❑ Your administration is easier as you ask for the specific information you want.

❑ The process is routinized making it familiar and therefore an easier task for people to register.

❑ It looks "professional."

❑ Most importantly, a form requiring sign-off by both the prospective participant and the line manager and asking for individual learning objectives will encourage proper discussion to take place between the employee and the manager before the training.

However, despite all these benefits, there will be times when people don't follow your "rules," either turning in an incomplete form or not using it at all. Never refuse a registration form just because others' administration is a bit sloppy. You can try to encourage more appropriate registration next time by offering the rationale or demonstrating the benefits, but at the end of the day you have a more important task than overseeing registration.

Finally, when people phone with registration questions, or your staff members need to contact participants for additional information, there is a real "moment of truth." The way in which your team handles these telephone calls is part of your "shop window." Make sure that people within your department conduct themselves according to the service message you want to give out. Remember the service maxim: "tough on standards, soft on people."

Managing Attendance

Many training managers seem to agree that it is useful to overbook, to ensure full course attendance. While it may be a practical way to keep courses from being cancelled, you should not overdo it, so that you have to regularly turn people away. Ultimately, people will stop registering. Aim for a system that is efficient without being bureaucratic—flexible without being slapdash. You can prevent people from dropping out of training events by personally advising them as to why their particular presence will be welcome.

Use personal telephone calls, e-mails, memos, or "late course announcements" to improve attendance levels, but *never* let "numbers" supersede the *appropriate* target population. If the wrong people are there, everyone loses.

Pre-course Information

Again, there is variety in how you communicate to people who have registered for your courses (e.g., small booklets, personal letters, etc.). The type of written communication you choose will depend upon how you want others to perceive your department. Remember that the tone of your written communications says a great deal about your image. One worldwide service company always sends participants a folder which includes enrollment instructions, pre-course readings, a list of course participants, course location, and other details. The folder comes in a special envelope with "IMPORTANT—REGISTRATION INFORMATION" printed on the front. Whatever your format, pre-course material should also include (where relevant)

❑ Event name, dates, times, and location

❑ Any pre-program preparation required

❑ Course site maps

❑ Airline/train schedules

❑ Taxi service phone numbers

❑ Parking details (especially in city locations)

❑ Contact telephone numbers at the course site (to be supplied to near and dear ones)

❑ Room facilities (phone, TV, etc.)

❑ A guide to local social, sports, and entertainment facilities

❑ Dress code—for day and evening when applicable

❑ Approximate course start and end times for each day

❑ Contact name and telephone number for any other information.

You may be able to think of other important information to include in the pre-course material. The important thing is to have a system, familiar to everyone at your end, so that whoever handles the administration for one event follows the same procedures for other programs.

Site Arrangements

Unless you are providing virtual training, you will be using a physical site for any group training and development program. Whether you use your company's training facilities or contract with an outside provider, there are important arrangements that must be made before every event in order to ensure "seamless" training provision. Even when you are in the business of booking your training rooms to others in your organization for their own use, you need to find out how they want the room set up and arrange to have things ready for them. This is some of the added value a training function can provide that can only improve their image in the eyes of the rest of the organization.

In-house

The room should be set up to reflect the learning activity and the group size prior to every event. Even if you are stuck with an immovable boardroom table, you will need to make decisions about equipment/handout placement, distribution of notepads, name-cards, handouts, etc. Leaving this to the last minute almost guarantees that at least one participant will arrive before the trainer has finished setting up.

Many training departments have developed forms on which the trainer can indicate room requirements. Copies go to the facilities people who set out the furniture, to catering, if appropriate, and to the training administrator whose job includes overseeing compliance with room set-up requests, as well as to the trainer. This is a way to avoid misunderstanding due to communication breakdowns. If you use this method, however, you should follow up from time to time to ensure the form has been received by the appropriate people and is continuing to meet their needs!

External sites (hotels, conference facilities, etc.)

When things do not go smoothly at an external site, your image is not enhanced just because everyone knows "it's not your fault." It is vital that a responsible member of your team meets with the duty manager or conference manager of the facility and stresses the importance of getting everything right. Nothing is worse than having to use up training time to deal with unnecessary complaints about the hotel.

Unfortunately, however, even the best site can become complacent if you return regularly.

With events that include overnight stays, take the time to sort out accommodation issues—registration and check-out procedures; whether rooms will be pre-assigned; the nature of the rooms (will some be single and others double? Will they be of equally high standard?); what types of charges are covered and what is the participant's responsibility; whether pets, partners, or children are expected and what has been planned for them; and so on. It can be a welcome extra for guests to find a personalized packet in their hotel room telling them where to meet, options for their free time, etc. One international company went so far as to have customized balloons in each room to set the tone for a creativity event. In another instance, the company placed "activity packs" in the participants' rooms during the first day of an HR strategy workshop, so that when participants returned to their rooms, they could work on some of the issues for the next day.

Wherever you hold your training events, the person responsible for the training should arrive at the training room *at least 45 minutes early* to make sure all details have been attended to. (*Always* make sure you have enough flipchart paper!) By the time participants arrive, the trainer should be calm and ready to welcome them. (The swan image is not at all out of place here.)

Registration

What happens when the participants arrive? So often, there is an expectation that participants are familiar with in-company training rooms, and trainers expect them to find their own way around. It is more professional to have a proper arrival system, with a clear effort to make participants feel welcome and special. If you use external consultants, you should have one of your staff on site to start things.

Paperwork should be minimal when people arrive—with modern computer equipment, there is no excuse for excessive duplication—but everyone should be identified by name and introduced to others. With large groups, think about using nametags, which participants complete, showing place of work, preferred name, and division, if your organization is large.

If you use external consultants, they will usually appreciate a list of participants, preferably with a bit of information about them (job title and department/location, etc.) and copies of any registration information or pre-course materials. But this is not just for the comfort of the consultants. With this basic information, they will then be able to greet participants and answer any early questions with some degree of ease, being seen as a representative extension of the training function rather than a totally separate (external) entity, i.e., presenting a "seamless" customer service.

Ensure a comfortable environment—designate informal areas where participants can sit and have conversations while enjoying refreshments. Indicate where smoking/non-smoking areas are located.

Hand out a "pack" on arrival—something for people to read, if they choose, while they wait for others to arrive. Encourage your trainers to circulate through the room, introducing themselves to new arrivals. All this builds a supportive environment, where your customer feels valued.

If the training site is in a hotel, the same things apply, but you will have a little less control. Allow time for people to check in before the course starts. Make sure the hotel has put up enough signs showing where the course is being held, and has provided the agreed amount of refreshments.

IN THE TRAINING ROOM

Starting with inner, non-cerebral needs, it is always preferable to have refreshments outside the training room, thus avoiding disruption and ensuring that the trainer and participants clear the room for a time. Even in air-conditioned hotels, training rooms can become oppressive, if there is no opportunity to leave them. There is the added benefit that people can stretch their legs, pick up messages, and look after personal comfort at their own pace. Don't push too hard for people to stick to unrealistic breaks—contract with them, to allow something reasonable.

At some point on the first day, ask participants if they are happy with the site arrangements, and monitor the catering carefully. The training rooms should be regularly replenished with water, soft drinks, mints, paper, pens, pencils, etc. If your training course does not offer free meals, make sure people know how to get to local restaurants. Allow enough time for people to relax at meals, but without losing impetus.

Needless to say, furniture should be of the highest possible standard, and all the equipment should be well-serviced and scrupulously clean, even if it does not represent the latest in state-of-the-art technology. Nothing looks worse than poorly presented visual materials—on paper or on screen.

COURSE MATERIALS

The key factor here is consistency. All your materials should be of a standard that reflects your brand of excellence. Handouts, course notes, ring binders, namecards, etc., will present a message to participants: Make sure it's the message you intend to send. Consider, for example, if you re-use tent cards by turning them over and writing names on the other side, does it look a) cheap? b) like you forgot to order more? c) like you're concerned for the environment?

All too often, handouts are compiled from a range of sources. Despite the existence of scanners, desktop publishing facilities, OCR software, etc., poor quality course materials (e.g., photocopies of different forms of type, crooked pages, and sometimes different types of paper) still crop up in training programs. What does this say to a participant—and anyone later who may look at the course notes? Answer: that not a lot of attention was directed at this learning activity. That translates into poor "customer care."

In addition to the course presentation, pay attention too to the style of your handouts. Verbose notes, running to several pages may be appropriate for a scientific setting, but not for a pragmatic business environment where bullet points—or perhaps pocket-sized, laminated cards—would be preferable. The needs of the customer (the learning need for the handout in this case) is key. Do they need to read it or refer to it later?

The same applies, of course, to other materials—overhead projection slides, computer projection screens, flipcharts, posters, etc. Many sources exist that give pointers on presentation of materials and visual aids, but however you decide to prepare and present your materials, you should keep in mind that these materials are one of the means of communicating with your customers—and communicating your image and your message. Make sure you and your training team (and any external consultants you use) are consistent with the message that is being delivered.

Getting It Right

The following checklist will help you get your training administration right, but like any service, don't stop there. Find ways to receive and capture feedback on your administration as well as on the services you provide. It will help you see from "the other side" and nip any problems in the bud. You may also be surprised at the little things people value and realize how some small detail can make a big difference to your customer. Aim for a total quality philosophy, one of continuous improvement in your department, with a bias for speedy action to deal with feedback.

Administrative Checklist

TELEPHONE

- ❏ Always covered (human or machine)
- ❏ Messages checked regularly—e-mail or voice mail
- ❏ Message retrieval and relay system implemented
- ❏ Calls returned promptly
- ❏ Published up-to-date lists of telephone numbers and e-mail addresses

TRAINING DIRECTORY (*if you have a good reason to produce one*)

- ❏ Up-to-date and accurate—regularly reviewed
- ❏ Well-produced, consistent with your chosen image
- ❏ An overview of your organization, training philosophy, and development mechanisms included
- ❏ Clear registration procedures provided
- ❏ Notes about key personnel and contact numbers included

COURSE ANNOUNCEMENTS AND PRE-COURSE INFORMATION

❑ Well-designed eye-catching format

❑ Straightforward and comprehensive—written with the recipient in mind

❑ Time(s), dates, and location(s) listed

❑ Enrollment or other information channels clearly identified

MEMOS, LETTERS, AND E-MAILS

❑ Composed with a consistent format, typeface, and style

❑ Standards understood by everyone in the department

❑ Written briefly and to the point

❑ Proofread by someone else—including e-mails

SITE ARRANGEMENTS

❑ Room and catering arrangements checked, communicated, and confirmed

❑ Liaison established with person who can get things done

❑ Checklists used to avoid missing details

❑ In case of residential or long-term events, daily meetings set up with site management

❑ Quality measured at every key point

REGISTRATION PROCEDURES

❑ Understood by everyone involved—including external providers

❑ Hassle-free and welcoming from the customer viewpoint

❑ Team trained to recognize the importance of getting off to a good start and setting the tone

COURSE MATERIALS

❑ Consistent standard and style

❑ Error-free

❑ Relevant to purpose; useful to the learner

❑ Carries the stamp of your image

❑ Procedure for periodic review of frequently used course materials

ACTIVITY

This team activity could result in several task or project assignments.

1. Rate each item on the Administrative Checklist as positive (+) or negative (-) in your current circumstance. If unsure, *consider the item from the customer viewpoint, or better yet, ask one or more of your customers for their opinion.*

     _____

     _____

     _____

2. Consider the causes and effects of each negative point. Note these.

     _____

     _____

     _____

3. What "successes" can you identify in the administrative area?

     _____

     _____

     _____

4. How can you build on the successes?

     _____

     _____

     _____

5. How can you eliminate setbacks?

     _____

     _____

     _____

SUMMARY

This chapter dealt with how administration procedures impact the overall success of the training strategy. It covers the "moments of truth" when staff talk to existing and potential customers, and it deals with the quality of the service we offer to back up the excellence of our training and development "products."

We provided practical tips for improving brochures, training materials and announcements, registration procedures, and training facilities. In addition, this chapter presented ways to follow up on customer comments or requests and to analyze the quality of the total administrative offering.

CHAPTER 9

Seamless Customer Service

No doubt you have brought in consultants for at least some part of your training and development activities. Many organizations rely heavily on external providers, believing it to be the best way to stay "lean" and have the expertise they want when they want it. Some have created alliances with outside agencies to manage the entire training and development process. One of the first such efforts was the Forum Corporation's alliance with DuPont where the corporate training function has been turned into a value-added business [1]. Other organizations are committed to keeping their training and development internal and will only call in a consultant when they have exhausted every in-house possibility. And obviously, there are approaches between these extremes. There are sound business reasons for relying to varying degrees on external providers for your training and development function. However, there are also marketing implications.

From a marketing standpoint, the use of external providers does say something to your customer. The important thing is to be in control of what it says. To be in control you must be absolutely clear as to why you are contracting out for the service, what you want from the consultant, and how you manage the relationship. From your customers' point of view, what should be important is performance improvement; from your point of view, the source (the external provider) of that performance improvement solution should be *seen* to be driven by your function.

WHY YOU BRING IN OUTSIDE HELP

There are several positive reasons for bringing in external consultants:

❑ Your own resources are fully stretched—an extra "pair of hands."

❑ You need a certain type of expertise not available within the organization. This can range from re-designing your performance appraisal system to setting up quality improvement teams.

❑ You feel an outsider will be more accepted in the particular instance (for example, to facilitate a high-level meeting where all internal people have a stake in the outcome or to lend credibility to a new procedure by virtue of experience with other organizations).

❑ An outsider can provide you with a service (for example, a training needs assessment) that is not biased from organizational pressures.

❑ You want a "big name" to impress or inspire the customer, often the only way "in" at very senior levels.

❑ You want external endorsement—in organizations where there is some insecurity as to the value of the training and development function, external consultants can help promote a sense of importance. Also, using an experienced consultant to support work you have initiated can give *you* the necessary confidence to continue.

❑ You don't want to be *directly* associated with the project, perhaps because it will be unpopular at first. For example, you might be instrumental in helping the organization move toward a new manufacturing process or in installing zero-based budgeting for planning. An organization that is experienced in implementing such systems may help increase acceptance of the project (and, as an impartial observer, will also be able to give you feedback about what you are doing). This is not cheating, just image protection. You can better use your facilitative skills to help the customers accept the benefits if you're not seen as the expert as well.

First, determine which of the reasons for using external help you are driven by. This will determine how you select and brief the consultant, and therefore, how they interact with your customers.

Selection Criteria

If you use a consultant simply to expand the resources of you and your team, you should employ the same election criteria as you would to recruit for a position within your department. The rest of the organization sees the consultant as part of the training function. It would be appropriate to fully immerse him or her in your department's functioning, letting him/her get to know your trainers, the work you are doing, etc., so they can operate as an extension of your current function.

If you are looking for expertise lacking internally (e.g., someone to devise and implement an attitude survey), you will, of course, check that the person has the required expertise. But it is often forgotten that outside consultants also carry the stamp of the training and development function when they work inside your organization. You also need to pay attention to how the individual fits with the image you have worked hard to promote.

If you choose to select a "big name," do you know who it will impress? How do you decide whether to go for credentials or personality (e.g., Harvard Business School vs. Tom Peters)? Is an international base important? Will your company see the academic/research base prominent in business schools as a plus or will they prefer a strong IT/systems base as found in one of the world-class accounting/consulting firms? If you use a market leader or high profile management institute, will your organization see this as "providing the best" or will they view it as frivolously spending money when the same—or perhaps more appropriate—service might be provided by a small firm or an independent consultant? And in the case of an independent, does the person have the right image? What will be more acceptable—"Sixties Chic" or "Business Crisp"? The point is that your choice invites value judgments from your customers. As we saw in Chapter 5, the context in which you provide customer solutions is extremely important. Which consultant you provide is a context issue and your sensitivity in selecting him or her will be perceived as part of the image people have of the training and development department.

You may not always be after "fit," however. You may purposely want to introduce a different type of role model into the organization to "jump start" a new change process. An example would be to install a new process that, by virtue of the consultant's outside experience, is immediately seen as credible. In this instance, the selection would have less to do with which business school or consulting firm the individual comes from, and more with the successes of similar projects in well-known organizations or with the well-publicized expertise established in that particular skill set.

If you do not have a final say in the selection of an external consultant, you should demonstrate to the person with the final say that your function has an important stake in the choice in light of the work you have done to determine the need for the consultant in the first place. You will need to build a proper case for those you have chosen, demonstrating to the decision-makers in business terms that "who" is as important as "what" and "how much," and justify your choice in terms of the needs and culture of the customer.

If, horror of horrors, you are *given* a consultant to work with, you should clear the air regarding who represents whom, the kind of relationship you expect to develop with the consultant, and how visible the training and development function's role should be to the customer during the intervention. Failure to attend to these matters can leave the training function vulnerable, its image tarnished, either from the direct customers if things go wrong, or from your sponsors if they see you to have no active role in managing the process.

Case in Point

Wanting to provide top-rate training for middle managers who possessed a range of skills, Judith, a training manager in a large distribution company, employed different external consultants for stress management and assertiveness programs. A subsidiary of the company was already running internal courses on these topics, using in-house trainers who had been externally trained. Trainers in Judith's department observed both courses and were very critical of the in-house events. However, line managers were critical of the external providers' "personal style."

A strong political agenda emerged within different parts of the company seeking to assert autonomy in choice of training providers. Within three months, Judith's boss suspended the use of external providers and appointed an operations manager to oversee in-house training.

Introducing the Alien

Once you have selected an external consultant(s), it is important that you properly introduce them into the organization. If they will be walking around various departments or interviewing staff to assess a problem or design a solution, it is up to you to "grease the wheels." Inform the departments why the consultant(s) will be working with them. It is a good idea to telephone and then follow up with a note or memo giving a little information about the consultant as well as the project. Failure to do this can leave you looking like you're not in control of the situation. Worse, all sorts of unsubstantiated stories can start, undermining the quality of *your* work. Your involvement, even if it's just a phone call, will also pave the way for further discussion should you want/need to check on how the consultant is doing.

On the other side of the equation, it is your responsibility to fully brief the consultant as to why you have hired him or her, what needs to be done, what problems you foresee, what support will be provided, whom to liaise with, any no-go areas or delicate situations, and how you expect the training function to be represented. Consultants will generally seek this information anyway, but it is surprising how often it is not forthcoming!

Managing Quality

It is not unusual for a training consultant to develop an ongoing relationship with an organization while working autonomously. It is also easy for a training manager to develop a sense of dependency on the consultant and, confident that he or she is doing a good job, get involved in other projects losing touch with the consultant's work. A certain level of continuous involvement is vital, however, if only to keep the consultant apprised of new issues or changes in the organization. If the consultant uses unfamiliar approaches, make sure your audience will relate to them and that they are consistent with or complement other concepts or approaches used within the organization. Monitor for quality and content any materials the external trainer provides.

Don't forget to attend to the administrative side of the introductions—provide your external trainer with necessary information about program registrants and their expectations of the program, and any assigned pre-course work. If you expect the trainer to use an external program site (e.g., hotel, conference facility, etc.), brief them thoroughly of your needs and expectations, and agree on responsibilities and levels of authority.

When you use an external consultant, you should cautiously monitor the project and his/her work. First, remain knowledgeable about how the project or projects are progressing so you can adequately represent the training function's contribution to the business. Second, maintain the standards set and nip in the bud any potential problems or veering off track.

Keeping on top of the situation is not just remedial. Some consultants can become so integrated with the work of the organization and are so popular with the employees, that the training function behind the consultant fades into the background. This is a time for some careful blowing of your own horn. You did well to choose so well. Keep it known that you and the consultant are "partners" in the activity.

Case in Point

In one fairly long-term relationship, an independent consultant provided all middle management training—about eight courses—for a large public sector company for three years. After two courses, the training manager, confident that the consultant was "on the same wavelength," stopped asking for copies of the training materials that the consultant developed and left the consultant to continue with the job. The only role the training manager had in the consultant's work was making the office photocopier available prior to each course. The training manager treated other consultants, who were providing more junior or senior management development, the same way. The consultants developed, produced, and distributed (to course participants) training materials without anyone in the organization checking for acceptability or consistency in content, style, or quality. In fact, there were no problems. However, once that training manager left the company and the particular consultants no longer had a relationship with the company, the training department had no files to refer to or build on. The marketing implications, not to mention the potential for other dire outcomes, are astonishing in this case.

Managing the Relationship

Just as managers' treatment of employees affects employees' treatment of customers, your relationship with the training consultant will affect the relationship between the consultant and your customer. If you want the consultant to carry a positive message about the organization and the training function, you will need to make the time to develop a quality relationship with the consultant. The best way to get this result is to view the consultant as a partner in the project(s). As with your "partnering customers," partnership here implies trust, sharing of relevant information and expectations, honest feedback, non-defensive receipt of feedback, fair treatment, and conscious allocation of time.

Financial arrangements—fair price for promptly completing work—will also affect the end result. Training consultants are not, nor should they be expected to be, doing you a favor. Even with the highest professional standards and with the best will in the world, working under less than satisfactory conditions will eventually effect the quality of their output.

> *"Why should I re-design the activities? They're not paying me enough for that."*

Case in Point

A giant national transportation company contracted a small consulting group to design and provide several training modules in certain management skills. After a successful first year, the company did not renew the contact with the consulting group. Instead, the transportation company's training director, who knew his company was in an advantageous position due to their prestigious name and the current lack of contract training work around, went directly to the firm's associates and offered them the work as "independents" (quoting a lower amount than the consulting group's fee but equal to the associate's fee). As interest in the training program was high, the company eventually asked the original consultant back as well—at the lower rate. Despite knowing what had transpired, the consultants continued to provide the training for another couple of years (while the quality of the training content remained constant). What subtle messages do you think the trainees got from the consultants about the training department? What are the ramifications—internally and externally—of the department's resulting image?

GET THE MOST OUT OF YOUR CONSULTANT–"PARTNER"

❑ Keep in touch through regular briefings—discuss and eliminate blockages and difficulties.

❑ Ask for (and listen to) feedback and observations they have made.

❑ Set standards and give feedback regularly, including the positive.

❑ Involve them in occasional planning and idea-generating sessions.

❑ Use their skills to add value to your administration.

❑ Involve them in marketing if they are willing.

SUMMARY

In this chapter we looked at the marketing implications of using external consultants and how this affects your perceived customer service. In particular, we looked at what the presence of external consultants says about the training function; how they extend (or replace) the image of the training and development function; and how you manage the process to get the best results for all involved.

NOTES

1. For a case history of DuPont's venture into insourcing, see *DuPont— Reinventing the Training Paradigm,* a leaflet published by the Forum Corporation, Boston, Mass., describing its first such strategic alliance, or visit the Forum website. At the time of this writing, the DuPont story can be found at: www.forum.com/CaseStudies/training_redesigned.htm.

CHAPTER 10

Expanding Your Horizons

Many training and development functions consider or actually experiment with offering their "products" or specialized expertise outside their own organization. It is a way to develop a reputation that raises your profile both outside and inside your organization. There are, of course, resource implications to consider—it is rare today for training and development functions to have any surplus capacity, but there are plenty of advantages and a number of possibilities, and once again this activity affects your customer focus in many ways.

Let's assume you want to look at this issue more closely, and can think of some ways to generate some specific resource. For example, you can use external consultants for the "routine" material so your own people can concentrate on special proprietary issues. What should you do next? First, you need to answer some basic questions:

❑ Where is your expertise? What does your department do particularly well that is unique? A SWOT analysis (listing your team's strengths, weaknesses, opportunities, threats) will help you answer these questions.

❑ Who else would benefit from your areas of expertise—other divisions, companies in your industry, industries or sectors?

Be aware that conflicting objectives may surface from this exercise. On the one hand, you are committed to a reputation for excellence providing services within your organization. On the other hand, you may be conscious of additional revenue you can generate to boost your budget, and the possibility of improving your market exposure and widening your customer-base. You may wish to draw attention to your expertise both within and outside your organization.

THE BENEFITS OF SERVING A WIDER PUBLIC

There are other important reasons why marketing externally can benefit you and your organization.

Over time, training departments can sometimes become set in their ways. Despite your best efforts, constant repetition of a series of training courses, which change little in the short-term, can lead to lack of interest from your trainers. We all know that most trainers want to gravitate towards "higher order" facilitative events as they gain experience. Giving them the opportunity to work in new environments with different audiences can enhance their skills and maintain their interest—a real development opportunity for training staff. Many training and development departments overlook the need to provide development mechanisms for the trainers themselves, and working outside the function is an ideal vehicle for personal development.

Your department can develop a reputation for being a good launching platform for people's careers. If your organization prefers "homegrown timber," working as a specialist internal consultant can effectively expose people from your department to senior managers. Alternatively, if your organization prefers flexible recruitment, with a regular throughput of talent, people will see the advantages the external opportunities offer them. Either way, you may be enhancing the reputation of your department as a good place to work—and so attracting the right talent to fill your trainer positions, in a kind of virtuous circle.

Providing training services to companies other than your own also sharpens commercial skills like financial management, contract negotiations, and public relations. The opportunity to promote and negotiate as an external provider can also add a new perspective when dealing with the external providers you employ. You and your people will understand more about the way in which external consultants can work successfully, and will bring this to the table when you evaluate them.

If you work in a quality-conscious environment where concepts like "Just In Time" inventory and supplier partnership are familiar, you may see opportunities for partnership that develop your external presence inside or outside the company.

Case in Point

One training manager intercepted the external supply chain in his organization by persuading the head office that all external suppliers should adopt common strategic approaches, training standards, and quality procedures. This suggestion led to a major initiative working in partnership with the head office and a representative group of the suppliers to develop quality standards, monitoring procedures, and techniques. The resulting training program was then made available to all current and future suppliers to the company.

More prosaically, consider bartering. Can you offer something you are good at to another department or organization in exchange for something they can do better than you? Especially when you are equipped with specialized skills, it is worth looking at your network of external contacts and considering what you have to offer that they would value.

Occasionally, opportunities to foray into the external market come along. Whether to take them further and go systematically outside your function depends on a careful analysis of your organization and an appreciation of your customers' perceptions.

THE "EXTERNAL" MARKET INSIDE

There are two ways to consider operating internally as an "extra" commercial endeavor. If you are part of a large organization, you can offer your expertise to other divisions or subsidiaries. Alternatively, in a smaller organization, you can offer support in a new range of services. For example, if you are known predominantly for training and development solutions, you can promote your presentation materials for meetings. The point is to "sell" the individual skills not always "seen" outside the training room (e.g., presentation coaching or materials development).

Offering your services in-house can suggest to people that you are approachable, flexible, professional, and helpful. If you do it well, you can gain a reputation for delivering the goods "right the first time, every time," and for adding value. You will develop a strong market presence which will increase your influence around the organization.

But beware! You might inadvertently gain a reputation for wanting to be involved in too much, for lacking focus, or for being known as the person that others unload their work on. To avoid this, think carefully about the way in which you will pitch your offer—concentrate on a limited range of specialist services or skills that are not generally available in your organization.

Case in Point

The HR director at a rapidly growing telecommunications consulting firm (60 employees) spotted a need for one-to-one coaching of many of the senior managers. Afetr discussing the benefits with the CEO, she collected details of several organizations who could provide this service and then, using those as a comparison, set up a separate coaching business within the existing HR function. She hired freelance counselors to provide the confidential service. She was able to charge a more favorable rate than would have been possible if contracted with a counseling firm to provide the service, and she boosted the range and reputation of her function at the same time.

SELLING TO THE OUTSIDE WORLD

You can also consider whether you have the capacity to sell outside your organization, in the commercial marketplace. This is certainly a way to increase your customer-base, generate additional revenue for your organization, and most importantly, from the perspective of this book, enhance your image. Here again, you will probably be offering something that is uniquely associated with what you do. Rather than attempt to compete with the generalist providers who devote 100 percent of their time to what you will be doing "part time," limit yourself to a special sector where you have something unique to offer, or to a specific area of skill in which you have developed a particular expertise or methodology.

In the U.S., one midwestern local government unit offers management training to local employers who lack the resources to hold their own training. They run a series of modular "open" workshops. Participants sign up for a series of six one-day workshops. This gives the public sector training department exposure to the commercial world, involves them in the local community, enhances the reputation of the government unit, and improves the image of the training function inside organizations.

A bank demonstrates another external sales method. It offers training in financial appraisal skills to other smaller banks in the area. Participants from the smaller banks join the training activities of the larger bank, and this gives employees of both banks an opportunity to learn from each other.

ACTIVITY

This activity will help you determine if your training department has any scope for external marketing.

Step 1: List those areas of expertise (or special experience or methodology) in which you think your training function excels, or will excel.

_____

_____

_____

Step 2: Now consider whether these areas or skills are widely available in your organization or in the outside world, or whether they are in short supply.

Skills	Widely Available	Short Supply

Step 3: Plot them on the diagram we suggested in Chapter 3.

High
Added Value

▼ LOW AWARENESS
▲ HIGH ADDED VALUE

▲ HIGH AWARENESS
▲ HIGH ADDED VALUE

Low
Awareness

High
Awareness

▼ LOW AWARENESS
▼ LOW ADDED VALUE

▲ HIGH AWARENESS
▼ LOW ADDED VALUE

Low
Added Value

If the skills or expertise you might offer have low market awareness and potentially high added value, marketing these skills is well worth looking at. Players in the market may not be ready, and you will have high impact. If there is high awareness and high added value, chances are that other training departments will already be offering these skills because the return is good. If you think you can stand the heat, it may be worth considering, but you will meet stiff competition. If there is high awareness and low added value, there is probably little to be gained from involvement in a very cutthroat and competitive market with poor returns for your efforts. Finally, if there is low awareness and low added value, the market will probably not want it.

Step 4: Judge where and how you might offer your chosen expertise. Will you be able to generate resources and senior management support for your objectives? How will you gain this necessary support? What will your organization gain?

_____

_____

_____

_____

Step 5: Finally, think about the messages you will be conveying to other parts of your organization. Will they enhance your reputation? Will you generate any unwanted rivalries or competition? If so, what will be the implications? What other factors should you consider?

_____

_____

_____

_____

Once you have completed the exercise, you will be able to draft a basic business plan which will help you sell your idea internally and serve as a guide when you begin to travel into the unknown territory of the external market.

Reaching Your Market

If you decide to market your department's expertise to outside organizations, you will need to establish yourself with your new market. Just like marketing internally, you must both be seen and let people know what you are offering. There is no one road to credibility, but the following will give you some starting ideas:

❑ Volunteer to speak at professional organization meetings and conferences or local radio and television programs. Use your own network or sign up with a speakers' bureau.

❑ Write articles for industry/professional publications; write a book. Send announcements of your articles or books to colleagues and potential customers; advertise them on a web site; contribute them to a professional online "list."

❑ Ask your marketing department to produce a brochure.

❑ Query the local Chamber of Commerce or an external business advisory service about ways to publicize what you are offering in your particular area.

❑ Publicize your successes as you begin to develop external business. (You can easily combine this idea with the first two ideas listed.)

❑ Finally, talk to others who have "gone public" and learn from their successes and mistakes.

A Few Words of Caution

Finally, we need to return to the ideas of relevance and real value, which were introduced earlier in Chapter 1. If you are considering external involvement, think carefully about the level at which you will offer your services—are you a discount or specialist store? It is all too easy to be drawn into providing "standard" training packages, especially when you are operating internally. What you offer outside will reflect on your organization as a whole, so take care to ensure it is current, useful, and appropriate to the target population, and of good value.

Opening your more generic internal training events to "outsiders" may initially sound like a good way to increase attendance, get more interaction, and bring in some revenue. But will your own population be enriched or put off by the presence of people from different organizations? Will their presence alter the success of the activity?

Whatever you do, you should seek to add value, and be perceived as doing so. Added value in this context will be the enhanced reputation of your organization, or the part of it in which you are based, as a consequence of what you do outside it.

SUMMARY

This chapter explores what happens when you develop a separate business from your organizational mandate—either selling new services within your organization or selling some of your existing expertise externally. The discussion included the benefits and drawbacks; what you should consider when determining if marketing your department's skills either internally or externally is for you; and ways to get started.

A Customer-Focus Checklist

This checklist will provide you with a way to quickly review where you are, and to remind you of what needs attention if the internal HR function is to remain viable.

Know Your Customers

❏ Prepare a customer map to identify your entire customer base.

❏ Differentiate your direct customers—your "sponsors" and your "influencers."

❏ Further identify your "influencers" under the headings of "champions," "blockers," and "doomsayers."

❏ Determine and code the "influence level" of each "influencer."

Set Your Priorities

❏ Complete a payoff matrix to determine how to balance your resources.

❏ Determine which priorities represent highest added value and lowest current awareness.

❏ Avoid promoting other people's ideas.

Plan Your Influence Strategies

❏ Plan how to involve and influence your champions.
❏ Carefully identify blockers and doomsayers and work out a strategy aimed at neutralizing their impact.

Determine the Context Needs

❏ Format: method, duration, group configuration
❏ Timing: busiest times, best time slots, etc.
❏ Environment: formality, special needs, status issues, etc.
❏ Style: trainer, learning method, labels

Image Work

❏ Assess your image in the organization.
❏ Determine the "right" image.
❏ Set standards to support your image and plan how to achieve them.

Check Your Marketing Focus

❏ Targeted benefits specific to customer groups.
❏ Communication links: face-to-face (one-on-one, meetings, events), telephone, paper, electronic (check your network).
❏ Added value for your department's reputation and the organization's.

Administration

❏ Standards set and agreed to
❏ Announcements
❏ Booking procedures

❑ Pre-course information

❑ Site arrangements

❑ Registration procedures

❑ On-site issues

❑ Materials

External Suppliers

❑ Clear reasons for using

❑ Selection criteria and processes

❑ Introduce them into the organization

❑ Make time for the relationship

❑ Managing quality

The Training Image Survey

You can reproduce and send the following survey questionnaire to some or all of your customer groups. As you will see, it is very short and should take only a few minutes of their time.

Even if you keep it anonymous, you may want to have the customer identify his/her department or part of the organization. This will help you analyze the results in terms of what part of your organization is receiving what messages.

As with any organizational survey, it is good practice to promise—and deliver—some type of response after you have digested the results.

The survey is designed so that you can do the scoring after the customer returns it to you. The second part of the survey (see page 132) is for that purpose. You will probably find it useful to do separate score sheets for each survey returned, and then group them in some logical way for your organization and plot them on a large version of the scale on a flipchart.

This training image survey is intended to assess others' perceptions of the training department. To complete it, give a rank order to each horizontal set of four words, assigning a 4 to the word you think best characterizes the training department, a 3 to the next most appropriate, etc. Be sure to assign a different rank number to each of the words in the set. *Ties are not allowed!*

Training Image Survey			
1. ___ supportive	___ accessible	___ organized	___ business-driven
2. ___ developmental	___ up-to-date	___ academic	___ leading edge
3. ___ informal	___ eager	___ cautious	___ inventive
4. ___ caring	___ flexible	___ efficient	___ professional
5. ___ receptive	___ reactive	___ systematic	___ strategic
6. ___ thought-provoking	___ practical	___ traditional	___ risk-taking
7. ___ helpful	___ outspoken	___ formal	___ influential

SCORING THE TRAINING IMAGE SURVEY

For each column on the survey, record the score for the item in the indicated row—not all rows are used. Then add up the scores in each section and record them under the headings.

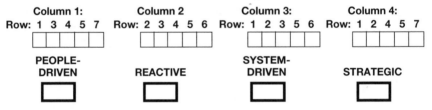

Column 1:	Column 2	Column 3:	Column 4:
Row: 1 3 4 5 7	Row: 2 3 4 5 6	Row: 1 2 3 5 6	Row: 1 2 4 5 7
PEOPLE-DRIVEN	REACTIVE	SYSTEM-DRIVEN	STRATEGIC

To see a visual representation of the survey results, place a dot on the appropriate axis for each of your four scores, and then connect the dots.

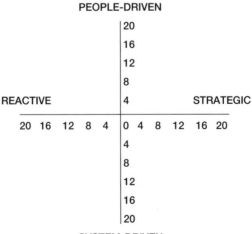

APPENDIX C

Trainer Styles

BACKGROUND

In the 1960s and 1970s, training moved gradually away from the world of talk and chalk, as trainers began to understand the role of the learner in the training process. Since then, there has been an explosion of interest in different ways to train people, responding to differences in learners.

Experiential activities are now the norm in most group training events—ranging from simple discussion groups to sophisticated simulations, games, or training outdoors. All these activities seek to make learning possible on different levels—not simply a cognitive experience.

Developing out of these early attempts to improve learning from training experiences, researchers Kolb *et al.* and Honey and Mumford (1992) and others have proposed models for the way people learn, which are widely referred to in training design. Figure C-1 illustrates Kolb's cycle of learning.

Kolb's model is now well known and has been widely re-interpreted and adapted. Both Kolb and Honey and Mumford have produced models of *learner styles* which suggest that people emphasize different aspects of the learning cycle, gaining more from some than others.

More recently, attention has returned to the interplay between organization, training event, trainer, and learner, drawing on more complex psychological models that take account of the roles played by the affective, cognitive, and psycho-motor domains of the learner

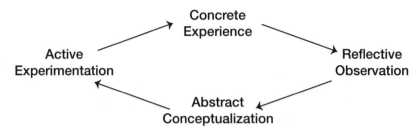

Figure C-1. Kolb's cycle of learning.

in the learning process. These approaches look more closely at the role of the trainer as part of the training interaction, not only in terms of the content delivery, but also in terms of the learning catalyst.

To take a simple example, ask yourself what role a trainer should play in a leadership development course? How much support is appropriate? This can be a complex issue, and is certainly influenced by a number of factors. Here are three:

1. Learner's perceptions of leadership
2. Organization's ways of expressing leadership
3. Trainer's views and preferences about leadership training

This takes us beyond the learning cycle into considerations of acting as role models to influence the learner within the learning context. What can the trainer do to help improve the likelihood of real learning? One way of becoming immersed in this area is to look at models of trainer styles and to assess the training in your own organization against one or both models.

Training Style Inventory

One model presented in the 1970s based on the thinking of Robert Mager, Carl Rogers, Douglas McClelland, and B. F. Skinner is called the Training Style Inventory and is freely available in the *1979 Annual Handbook for Group Facilitators* (originally published by University Associates and now available through Jossey-Bass/Pfiffer). Richard Brostrom developed the inventory, which is based on two dimensions: Cognition and Locus of Control, and results in four styles: Functionalist, Structuralist, Behaviorist, or Humanist.

The Cognition continuum moves from *Holistic/Sense Perception*, explained as dealing with wholes, moving spontaneously, and generally right-brain oriented to *Analytic Verbal*, which refers to rationally-minded, systematic and sequential, or generally left-brain dominated.

Locus of Control could be *Internal*, demonstrating a preference for independence, autonomy, and the chance to control one's own destiny, to *External*, preferring to respond to external forces or guidance from others. The four scales that emerge from either of the two dimensions are:

1. **Behaviorist:** Supportive with emphasis on controlling and predicting the learner and learning outcomes; precise and deliberate; the "doctor" model

2. **Structuralist:** Directive with planning, organizing, presenting, and evaluation tightly constructed for best effect; the "expert" style

3. **Functionalist:** Assertive, problem-focused, challenging, confrontational at times, a task-driven coaching style

4. **Humanist:** Reflective, stressing authenticity, equality and acceptance; a counseling approach.

The FADE Model

David Cleeton developed a more recent model of trainer styles, FADE [1] (© 1993 Cleeton-Watkins Associates, Wales, Great Britain), which links training preferences to learning styles. As it is not widely available, we will describe it more fully here.

This model suggests that trainers will exhibit preferences in the way they interact in the training room, based upon value judgments about the worth of different interventions. The model uses two dimensions:

1. **Content–Process:** This is the extent to which a trainer will express a concern for either the process or the content. This dimension may manifest itself in a cognitive acknowledgment about the value of facilitative interventions while using them to draw a training group along a pre-determined path (emphasizing content). Alternatively, and more extremely, the trainer may

avoid any intervention in group processes altogether (content again). By contrast, some trainers are prepared to sacrifice "the agenda" to develop a group interaction that looks fruitful (emphasizing process).

2. **Involved–Uninvolved:** This dimension identifies how a trainer might express a concern for personal involvement within group processes. It may manifest itself in a concern that the trainer is leader, encouraging followership (at a process level). Or, there may be a tendency for the trainer to feel a strong need to help with resolving problems (at a content level).

The FADE model offers four scales to describe these preferences:

1. **Facilitators** separate their own needs from those of the group. They are primarily concerned with group process and feelings. They have less need to feel involved with group activity, and prefer to help others to discover for themselves. They will provide advice if asked, preferring a counseling style of interaction with individuals. They are supportive of exploration and comfortable with uncertainty and with unstructured experiences like T-groups. They may believe that people learn best from interaction with others in a random or unpredictable way and will consequently lean towards experiential approaches to training. Consequently, they may dislike working with didactic material, acting as expert, or participating highly structured activities. They are prepared to take risks, and their focus is on the uniqueness of the self. In their interactions with others they are likely to explore new ideas by encouraging others to share their feelings and by listening actively.

2. **Activators** work with the group toward mutually agreed goals. They seek to build strong relationships with and within their training group. Their primary concern is with people and their feelings. They will tend to encourage involvement from everyone in a training group and feel slightly uncomfortable with people who tend to sit back. They believe that people learn best from working jointly with other people who can provide constructive feedback on performance. They feel most at ease when encouraging a group in joint problem-solving activities and may offer

unsolicited advice and guidance if they believe the group might benefit. They are comfortable with experimentation and provide the group with strong encouragement to achieve, but they may prefer this to be within a structured experience with a defined range of possible outcomes. Within these constraints, they are prepared to accept some risks as part of the learning process. Interactions will tend to be open and friendly with encouraging nonverbal cues.

3. **Demonstrators** encourage learners to accept their views and methods. They tend to focus on practical application. They are comfortable when advising, prompting, or showing people what is required, and encourage people to try things out by acting as a role model for the group. They will happily supply information, but are less happy when things stray into the theoretical or abstract, preferring to deal with practical experience as suggested by what has worked for them or others they have learned from. They can be uncomfortable with untried approaches, preferring to work toward clearly defined objectives, and will avoid risk by adhering to an agreed training structure until they are persuaded there is a better way by direct experience. They may believe that people learn from attempting things differently, and that this is best achieved by observation, imitation, and practice, combined with expert coaching. They will value their relationship with the group and will seek an atmosphere of active enthusiasm.

4. **Educators** provide information for subsequent evaluation. They are principally concerned with increasing people's knowledge and improving judgment. They are comfortable with didactic and structured approaches to training and may have some difficulty accepting that an entirely experiential approach to training might be valid for some learners. They will tend to see their role as a supplier of knowledge and methods for learners to work with. They may believe that people learn best by listening to the expert, posing questions, and drawing what they need from the accumulated expertise they are offered. They will see each learner as an individual, and consequently may be less concerned with group processes. They will avoid risk and feel uncomfortable if learners appear not to understand what is being said or when training sessions stray from the previously defined learning goals.

Figure C-2 shows how the four styles of interaction fit together.

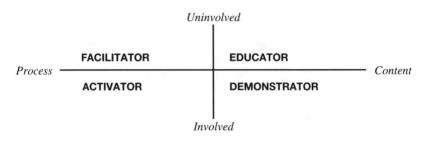

Figure C-2. Model of how the four styles of interaction fit.

NOTES

1. The FADE Model was developed by David Cleeton, Cleeton-Watkins Associates, Assessment Services, Annedd Darren, Bwlech, Brecon, Powys LD3 7RX, Wales, United Kingdom; Fax: +44 1874 730891.

Developing Your Network

This simple activity can be completed in about 15 minutes. Anyone who needs to influence other people in the workplace might look at it from time to time, to see how their network is developing. Here's what you do:

1. Gather together some large sheets of paper (perhaps from a flip chart), some scrap paper, some square sticky notes, a pair of scissors, and a pen or pencil.

2. On a piece of scrap paper, write down all the people or groups your department relates to at work. Devise a code—numbers, letters, colors, etc.—to indicate the level of importance this relationship has for your impact on the organization.

3. Take a large sheet of paper and draw a circle in the middle to signify your department or team.

4. Now draw two or three larger concentric circles around it to show levels of accessibility to you. Fo example, the first circle would be for those areas you relate to frequently or those people or groups who are physically near you; those you have least access to would be in the outer circle or around the edge.

Now Diagram Your Network Like This

1. For those persons or groups, whom you coded as important to your success, in any way—write their names on individual sticky notes.

2. Now spread out your notes and sort them according to the level of importance. For the least important, cut the size down to about a quarter of the original. As the level of importance increases, cut the notes larger, until you reach the most important, which will be uncut.

3. Place these notes around your own note—closer if the relationship is close or easily accessible, further away if it is not. Adjust as you go. Your "network map" may look something like Figure D-1, which shows that those with the highest level of importance, the most influential, are the least accessible. The next task would then be to find specific ways to make other persons or groups more accessible.

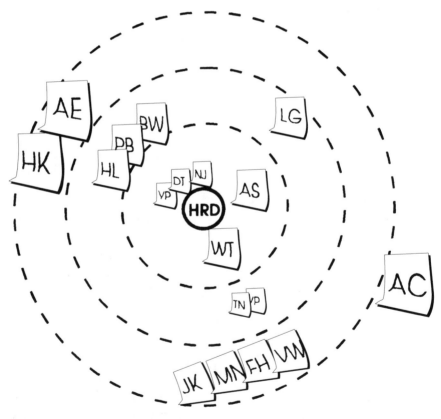

Figure D-1. A network map.

Further Reading

Marketing is not really something you can learn by reading. The following publications will round out many of the areas touched on in the text and will be useful for the reader who wishes to delve deeper into related areas.

The Training and Development Function

Robinson, Dana Gaines and Robinson, James E. (1996) *Performance Consulting*, San Francisco, CA: Berrett-Koehler.

Rothwell, William J. and Kazanas, H. C. (1993) *Human Resource Development: A Strategic Approach*, Amherst, MA: HRD Press.

Ulrich, Dave. (1996) *Human Resource Champions*, Harvard Business School Press.

Training Needs Assessment

American Society for Training and Development. (1992) *Trainers Tool Kit Needs Assessment Instruments*, Alexandria, VA: ASTD.

Training Evaluation

Kirkpatrick, Donald L. (1994) *Evaluating Training Programs—The Four Levels*, San Francisco, CA: Berrett-Koehler.

Newby, Tony. (1992) *Training Evaluation Handbook,* London, England: Gower.

Phillips, Jack L. (1996) *Accountability in Human Resource Management,* Houston, TX: Gulf Publishing Co.

MARKETING

American Society for Training and Development. (1986) *How to Market Your Training Programs,* Info-Lines, No. 26, Alexandria, VA: ASTD.

Cathcart, Jim. (1990) *Relationship Selling: The Key to Getting and Keeping Customers,* New York, NY: Perigee.

Whiteley, Richard and Hessan, Diane. (1996) *Customer-Centered Growth,* Addison-Wesley.

Yohahem, Kathy C. (1997) *Thinking Out of the Box,* New York, NY: Wiley & Sons.

CREATIVE THINKING

Buzan, Tony. (1982) *Use Your Head,* London, England: Ariel Books, BBC.

Russell, P. (1979) *The Brain Book,* London, England: Routledge & Kegan Paul.

Robinson, Alan G. and Stern, Sam. (1997) *Corporate Creativity: How Innovation and Improvement Actually Happen,* San Francisco, CA: Berrett-Koehler.

LEARNING STYLES

Honey, Peter and Mumford, Alan. (1992) *The Manual of Learning Styles* (updated issue) and *The Manual of Learning Opportunities,* UK: Peter Honey Publications.

Kolb, David, Rubin, I. M., and McIntyre, J. M. (1974) *Organizational Psychology, An Experiential Approach,* N.J.: Prentice-Hall.

Index